Sir William Mitchell Acworth

The railways of Scotland

Sir William Mitchell Acworth

The railways of Scotland

ISBN/EAN: 9783743346147

Manufactured in Europe, USA, Canada, Australia, Japa

Cover: Foto ©ninafisch / pixelio.de

Manufactured and distributed by brebook publishing software (www.brebook.com)

Sir William Mitchell Acworth

The railways of Scotland

Sir William Mitchell Acworth

The railways of Scotland

PREFACE.

The present work, though it would claim to be regarded as a book complete in itself, is, to this extent, a supplement to the larger book which I published last year on the Railways of England—that it avoids dealing with matters which are there described, and that it owes its existence to the favour with which the public received its elder brother.

Once more I have to acknowledge my obligations to the officials of the different lines for the ready assistance they have given me, and for the information which in almost every case they have freely placed at my disposal. More especially I must express my gratitude to Mr. George Graham, who, as one of Joseph Locke's assistants, started the first passenger train upon the Caledonian Railway, of which for seven-and-thirty years he has now been chief engineer, not only for a copy of his privately printed work on the origin of the Caledonian, but also for the unwearied kindness which has opened to me the stores of railway knowledge garnered for half a century by a marvellously accurate and retentive memory. To Mr. Drummond also, the locomotive superintendent of the same line, who has placed unreservedly at my disposal a large mass of curious and interesting old railway documents collected by him, I would tender my most hearty thanks. Not a little of the detail in the first chapter has, I may add, been filled in by tradition, handed down in my own family from the time when my grandfather was one of the original promoters and directors of the Monkland and Kirkintilloch Railway. To Mr. Arrol also, the builder of the Forth Bridge, I must express my thanks for the kindness which led him, not only to explain to me some of the methods adopted in the execution of his wonderful work, but also to look through and correct the proof sheets of what I have written on the subject.

CONTENTS.

I.—SOME FRAGMENTS OF ANCIENT HISTORY.

Competition Ubiquitous and Universal—An Eighteenth Century Waggon-way—Self-moving Engines—The Forth and Clyde Canal—A Confounded Gash in a Hill—A Barge Railway—The Monkland and Kirkintilloch—Primitive Railway Working—The Monkland Railway—A Bank Holiday in 1834—Growth of Passenger Traffic—Steam Road-Carriages—A "One-Horse" Road—The only Railway to Scotland—Annandale v. Nithsdale—The Beattock "Bank"—The Projectors of 1846—The Caledonian Railway 1

II.—THE OUTLOOK FOR THE FUTURE.

Earthen Pots and Brazen Vessels—The Reading and Bath Direct—The Forth Bridge—Cantilevers not Arches—Joining the Girders—The Earlier Schemes—The Approach Lines—Glenfarg, Old and New Style—"Magnificent, but not War!"—Breakfasting at Inverness—The Unique Railway Phenomenon—Permutations and Combinations—Mugby Junction—The Railway Luxemburg—The Dantonesque North British—The West Highland—Cornering the Highland—The Aviemore Line—A Railway Battle Royal—The East Coast Attitude—A Policy of Retaliation 39

III.—SOME MODERN SPECIALITIES.

Greenock and Gourock—The Race to the Coast—Eleven Trains and Thirteen Boats—Quantity no less than Quality—Halfpenny a Mile Fares—A Problem of the Future—A Triumph of Organization—A Lesson for Londoners—A Vote of Confidence—Profaning the Name "Express"—Growth of Glasgow Traffic—Avoiding Useless Expense—The Waverley Route—In the Brake of a Cattle Train—The Edinburgh Cattle Market—The Mushroom Company, Limited 83

IV.—THE GREAT NORTH AND THE HIGHLAND.

A Scotch Great Eastern—The Great North Lightning Express—The Deeside Line—Herrings, Whales, and Convicts—Whalebone *au Naturel*—A Herring Store—Soles at £3 a Ton—Working the Fish Traffic—Observation Waggons—The Strathspey Line—The Highland Mail Service—A Granite Quarry—A Great Beef Factory—"Accommodation" Trains—Services in the Far North—An Impenitent Sinner—Safety *versus* Convenience—Preposterous Precautions—The Highland Locomotives—The Break-down Train—The Automatic Snow-Fence . 116

V.—MINOR BUT MERITORIOUS FEATURES.

Return Tickets for Sheep—The West Coast Fishery—Train-Tablet Improvements—Changing Tablets at Speed—The Ayrshire and Wigtownshire—Portpatrick and Stranraer—Working for a Dividend—Abolition of Second Class—Theory and Practice—Liberality to Customers—Carriage Heating—Number 123—A Batch of New Engines—The Grease Factory—Traders' Waggons—Electric Lighting—The Prospects of the Future 158

INDEX 193

THE RAILWAYS OF SCOTLAND.

I. SOME FRAGMENTS OF ANCIENT HISTORY.

THE most obvious and important difference between the railways of Scotland and the railways of England, taking the two systems as a whole, is suggested by the first glance at the map of them given in *Bradshaw*. Railways in England are many, in Scotland comparatively few. With three-fifths of the area of the larger country, Scotland has little more than one-fifth of the railway mileage, and even of this scant total of some 3000 miles, not much over one-third is double line, while in England the proportion is the other way. In fact, though the traffic carried over its railways and its total railway capital are almost three times as great, in mere length of miles Scotland is but little ahead of Ireland. A comparison, however, between Scottish and Irish railways would be evidently unprofitable. In one respect only can the latter claim pre-eminence; though they have only a third of the traffic, they employ four times as many boards of directors to look after it.

Another point may be noticed. Even round London itself the net-work of lines is scarcely closer woven than it is round Newcastle, or Leeds, or Manchester, and two or three more provincial towns. In Scotland, with the exception of three or four main routes, running, roughly speaking, north and south, and by no means as crowded as they are important, the whole traffic is concentrated in the belt which stretches across the centre of the country from sea to sea. Take out Ayrshire, Renfrew, Lanark, and Midlothian from the map of Scotland, and you withdraw half the population and three-quarters of the traffic. Prolong the belt north-eastwards through Stirling and Fife to Forfar and Aberdeenshire; and what remains of Scottish traffic—it consists for the most part of fish, flesh, and fowl (or at least grouse), for the good red herring mostly goes by sea—is hardly worth fighting for.

But Scotch railways deprived of the opportunity of fighting would scarcely know themselves again. We talk of fierce competition in England, and compared to the sluggish monopolies of France or Germany competition in England is doubtless keen enough, but even in Lancashire itself there is here and there such a thing as non-competitive traffic.

In Scotland there is practically none. Probably the two most important places dependent entirely on a single company are Ayr and Oban. To Ayr the Caledonian already has running powers *via* Muirkirk, which it can exercise when it pleases, and it is an open secret that it means before long to apply for leave to construct an independent line along the coast from Glasgow; while it is equally certain that, if the North British has not a share in the Oban traffic before many years are out, it will at least not be for want of trying to get it.

It is then in universal and ubiquitous competition that the keynote to the Scottish railway system is, I think, to be found. And fierce as the battle is at this moment, it is likely to wax yet fiercer in the immediate future. The gap that has hitherto parted Linlithgow from Fife is now closed up; after seventy years of projects and projectors the Forth has at length been successfully bridged, and in the coming summer we shall doubtless see a determined effort made by the North British and its allies to dislodge the Caledonian Railway from the pre-eminence it has hitherto held both at Perth and Aberdeen. Nor is this all. The lust of battle, in the language of Horace, *crescit indulgens sibi.* Scotland, as has been said, is wide, and in most parts railways are few and far between. Last session Parliamentary sanction was given to a scheme, almost as ambitious as that of the Forth

Bridge itself. A new West Highland line, guaranteed and worked by the North British, is to be constructed from the Clyde, near Helensburgh, northwards along Loch Lomond, across the desolate moor of Rannoch, to the banks of the Caledonian Canal. For the present its terminus is Fort William; but it is impossible to think that its promoters will rest satisfied till they obtain extensions both to Inverness and the Ross-shire coast.

On the opposite side of the country the Great North of Scotland is pressing forward Bills for a new line from Elgin to Inverness, and also for a ferry service across the narrow entrance of the Inverness Firth and the Beauly Basin, so as to tap the traffic of Cromartie and Ross-shire, before ever it reaches Inverness at all. And much more important than either of these schemes is the agreement for amalgamation between the Glasgow and South Western and the North British. If the amalgamation be sanctioned by Parliament, we shall see ere long a fight such as this generation has not known. The united Company—operating, it is true, on exterior lines, but with the great forces of the Midland, the Great Northern, and the North-Eastern behind it—will advance simultaneously from the east and the west to do battle with the Caledonian, strong in its central position and its intimate alliance with the great North-Western interest, for the supremacy of Scotland.

the *tapis* at present. For if with its right hand the Great North is making a fierce onslaught on the Highland, it is simultaneously holding out its left hand and inviting that company to a conference to discuss the possibility of uniting the two concerns. What it all means the future will show, but if it means peace and friendship between the Highland and the Great North, then one will be inclined to think that there must have been more of the Kilkenny cats left than is commonly understood to have been the case.

But of all this more anon. Meanwhile we may notice that the Scotch railway system had already attained its majority before ever anything had been heard—not of competition only but actually of through traffic at all. The earliest Scotch lines, more than one of which is entitled to look down not merely upon the Liverpool and Manchester, but even upon the Stockton and Darlington itself as a mushroom upstart, were constructed simply for local traffic, mainly, of course, that in iron and coal. The nucleus of the Clydesdale Junction, an extension of the original Polloc and Govan Railway, now itself absorbed into the Caledonian, and forming the present access from London and the South to the Central Station in Glasgow, was a tramway, or "waggon-way," as it is called on the old maps, which, as early at least as 1778, ran from the collieries of Little Govan to the Clyde at Springfield, a point below the town where now the docks end, only to give place to the great shipbuilding yards, which skirt the downward course of the river for miles. The Kilmarnock and Troon line, the main road to-day between Ayr and the South, obtained its Act of Parliament in 1808, and was opened for traffic in 1811. It is thus described in Aiton's Agricultural Report of Ayrshire for that year, which was evidently written when the line was on the eve of completion:

"The distance from Troon Harbour to Kilmarnock is somewhat more than 10 miles, the total rise from Troon to Kilmarnock being 80 or 84 ft. which is 1 in 660. The iron rails are 3 ft. long, 4 inches broad in the flat part, about 4 inches in the deepest part of the parapet, weighing each about 40 lbs.; they are 4 ft. apart, and there is nearly 4 ft. between the two roads to allow the wagons to pass freely. The rails are fixed to square blocks of stone by nails driven into oaken pegs, 6 inches long and $1\frac{1}{4}$ inch in diameter, fixed into the blocks of stone. The railway crosses the Irvine by a bridge of 4 arches, one of them on dry land to make up the road, each of 40 feet span and rising 25 above the surface of the river. Raising, boring and carriage of the blocks will cost about 6d. each, and upwards of 70,000 are to be used in the railway. The same number of rails of cast iron at 40 lbs. each will weigh 1250 tons, which, with the carriage from Glenbuck foundry, will at present prices cost, when laid down on the road, £30,000. It is said that a horse will draw upon the railway when finished from 10 to 12 tons towards Troon, and from 8 to 10 towards Kilmarnock. Each wagon when loaded weighs about 1¼ ton. A horse at this time, October 28, 1811 draws two wagons loaded, at the rate of 2 miles an hour."

The construction of the Troon and Kilmarnock line fired the inhabitants of Dumfries to demand a railway from Dumfries up Nithsdale, in order to bring down coal from the Sanquhar collieries. It was proposed that it should be built so as to be used by trucks carrying 12 to 15 cwt. apiece, with bodies which could be taken off the wheels and slung, if necessary, on board canal boats. The Dumfries people got their line, but they had to wait thirty years for it, and when it came it was rather, to use the French phrase, as a *route nationale* than merely a *chemin d'intérêt local*. But in the interval not a few other local lines were projected and carried out; for one there was the Edinburgh and Dalkeith, which obtained in 1826 an Act authorizing the promoters "to make and erect so many self-moving, commonly called locomotive, engines as they may think proper," and requiring the owners of wagons using the line "in all cases to put their names outside." Apparently, however, the company did not think proper to avail themselves of their right to erect self-moving engines, for down to as late as the year 1845, passengers on the Edinburgh and Dalkeith were drawn by horses to the foot of an incline, and then the carriages were attached to the ropes of a stationary engine. Now-a-days passengers get to Dalkeith by a branch off the main Waverley line, and the old road, up which, with its gradient of 1 in 50, some seven or eight trucks are as much as an engine can take, is closed entirely as far as passengers are concerned. A somewhat similar thing has happened in the case of the Dundee and Newtyle, another line which is more than sixty years old. As originally built, it ran straight up the face of the hill out of Dundee. Locomotives being, however, less accommodating than stationary engines in the matter of gradients, the modern line winds round the side. But though the distance is doubled, probably the time occupied varies in an inverse ratio.

Much more important, however, than these latter lines were the railways in the immediate neighbourhood of Glasgow. It is difficult to realize that Glasgow, spite of its mediæval archbishopric and mediæval university, its associations with Queen Mary and the Covenanters, with Prince Charlie and Rob Roy, who to us are heroes of romance at least as much as historical characters, is an essentially modern town. If proof were needed of Glasgow's unimportance even so recently as a century back, it might perhaps be found in the fact that the main channel of the Forth and Clyde Canal, which, though begun in 1768, will only this year celebrate its centenary, avoided the town altogether; and in the further fact that the undertaking, which was estimated to cost no more than £150,000, in spite of its association with the great names of Brindley and Smeaton, dragged on year after year for lack of funds, and was only finally completed with the aid of a grant from the public purse.

The Forth and Clyde Canal has now passed into the possession of the Caledonian, so it would have in any case a natural claim to mention in an account of the Railways of Scotland. But it has a better title than this. It was in order to get coals down from the Monkland Coalfield to the Canal for shipment that the first public railway in Scotland, the Monkland and Kirkintilloch, was constructed. But before we come to this railway let us go back half a century and see what the Monkland Coalfield was. By doing so we shall be brought in contact with a name greater even than those of Brindley and Smeaton, the name of James Watt himself. In the year 1769 "the encreasing price and scarcity of coal" in Glasgow roused its citizens to consider whether a navigable canal could not be formed from the Monkland "Coalierys to the city." Watt was called in to advise. He prepared a scheme for a canal 16 feet wide at the bottom, sloping to 23 feet width at the top, with a mean depth of $4\frac{1}{4}$ feet of water. The canal was to be 10 miles in length, and to descend from its starting-point "one mile above Cotes Bridge" (*sic*), where it would be 266 feet above the level of the Clyde, through a series of twenty locks to the outskirts of Glasgow. But the cost of this scheme was estimated at £20,000, a charge which Watt himself felt to be prohibitory. Accordingly he submitted at the same time a second scheme. By stopping a mile short of Glasgow on the high ground to the north-east, he found it possible to dispense with the locks, and so, after allowing £1000 for Parliamentary expenses and contingencies, to bring down his revised estimate to £9653 10s.

For the mile from the terminus of the canal into the city, the carriage of the coal was to be effected by a "wagon way" down a steep slope, and the calculations as to the use to be made of this convenience are so curious as to be worth recording. It is estimated, says Watt, that the Glasgow consumption of coal amounts annually to 70,000 tons. Of this the Monkland district is said to be capable of supplying 20,000. Assuming the cost at the pit's mouth to be 10*d.* per cart of 7 cwt.

—it gives one an idea of the state of the roads and the power of the Clydesdale horses of the time to read that the normal cart-load was 7 cwt.—the coal should be delivered to the consumer in Glasgow at 20*d.* per cart, or 5*s.* per ton. He added that, supposing the consumption to increase and the canal to become inadequate for its traffic, the right way to obtain relief would be to deepen it, and so permit the use of larger barges than the 30-inch draught vessels which he proposed to employ in the first instance. "The advantage of fords for communication of lands will indeed be lost, but these can be supplied by bridges."

Two years after Watt's survey an Act was obtained "for making and maintaining a navigable cut or canal and wagon-way from the coalleries in the parishes of Old and New Monkland to the city of Glasgow." Watt was appointed to superintend the construction. His salary was £200 a year, and for this sum he had, with the assistance of a single clerk, to perform the various functions of surveyor, engineer, superintendent of works, and treasurer. According to a letter of his quoted by Mr. Smiles, he had 100 men employed under him who, as a result of twelve months' working, "made a confounded gash in a hill." The hill referred to is unquestionably Blackhill, some three miles out of Glasgow, where the gash may still be seen. For the scheme as actually carried out appears to have been of the nature of a compromise between Watt's two proposals, and at Blackhill the canal descends towards Glasgow down a steep slope through a series of four deep locks in close succession. But the activity of Watt and his hundred men did not last long. A commercial panic in 1772 put a stop to the works, and Watt lost his place. Ten years later the bankrupt and unfinished concern was bought by the great Glasgow firm of William Stirling & Sons, who not only completed the canal, but by a new undertaking, known as "the Cut of Junction," carried it on through the outskirts of Glasgow to Port Dundas, where it united with the Glasgow branch of the Forth and Clyde Canal. Thus in the year 1790 the Monkland Collieries first obtained their access to the sea.

Like the main undertaking, of which it forms a feeder, the Monkland Canal has long been the property of the Caledonian Railway. Though its traffic has now shrunk to but small dimensions, at one time it must have been very considerable. Not only was it found necessary to duplicate the series of locks at Blackhill, but also a supplementary route was provided in a most ingenious fashion for the return of the empty barges. On the face of the hill alongside the locks, a wide road has been constructed, sloping downwards at an angle of some 30° from the canal at the top to the canal below. On this road is laid a double line of broad-gauge rails. Two iron tanks or caissons, propped up at the lower end so as to keep the water within at a level, and large enough to contain a barge afloat, ran up and down these rails on ordinary railway trucks. A caisson coming up with an empty barge was balanced against a caisson going down filled only with water, the deficiency in lifting power being made good by the help of a stationary engine. Within the last two or three years, however not only has the use of this incline been abandoned, but one of the two series of locks has been closed, as it is found that a single set (with four lockmen where formally a dozen were employed) is sufficient to accommodate the rapidly diminishing traffic. It is often said that railway companies should not be permitted to own canals, and that, when they do possess them, they use their powers to suppress competition, so it may be added that, if any person or persons wish to obtain possession of the Monkland Canal in order to reduce the coal rates into Glasgow, there would probably be little reason to apprehend any factious opposition on the part of the Caledonian Company.

But we must get back from canals, which after all are but a very small item in the vast mass of miscellaneous property—docks, hotels, steamboats, and so forth—which has come into the possession of modern railway companies, and devote our attention to railways proper. As already mentioned, the first Scotch railway was the Monkland and Kirkintilloch. It obtained its Act of Parliament in 1824, and was opened for traffic in October 1826, one year later than the Stockton and Darlington. In one respect it is evident that its promoters had profited by Northumbrian experience. Readers of Mr. Smiles's 'Life of Stephenson,'—and who has not read it?—will remember that the original Stockton and Darlington Act of 1821 contained no power to use locomotives, or to carry passengers, and that these defects were only remedied by an Amending Act in 1823. The original Monkland and Kirkintilloch Act contained this clause: "And be it further enacted that it shall and may be lawful to and for the said Company of Proprietors, or any Person or Persons authorised or permitted by them, from and after the passing of this Act, to make and erect such and so many locomotive or moveable Engines as the said Company of Proprietors shall from Time to Time think proper and expedient, and to use and employ the same in and upon the said Railway, for the purpose of facilitating the Transport, Conveyance, and Carriage of Goods, Merchandize, and other Articles and Things upon and along the same, and for the Conveyance of Passengers upon and along the same." This Act authorized the expenditure of £32,000; but in the preamble of an Amending Act passed nine years later it is stated that "the said Railway has been made and executed at an Expense considerably exceeding the Amount originally estimated for completing the same."

As opened for traffic in October 1826, the railroad was 10 miles in length. It was a single line, with passing-places at intervals. Within ten years, however, the growth of the traffic compelled the directors to double it throughout. There was a fall of 127 feet from the starting-point "on the March or Division between the Lands of Palace Craig and Cairnhill in the Parish of Old Monkland" to the terminus at the Kirkintilloch basin on the Canal, or, in other words, a favourable gradient averaging about 1 in 400 throughout. At the outset the proprietors do not appear to have availed themselves of their privilege of using moveable engines, for we read that "one horse draws four wagons = 12 tons, and returns with the empty wagons, making three journeys in two days." The whole expense amounts to 1s. 2d. per ton, made up as follows: haulage, 5d.; railway dues, 7d.;—the statutory maximum under this head was 1s. 8d.—wagon hire, 2d. On one occasion it is reported that the horse "Dragon" drew 14 wagons = 50 tons, from Gargill Colliery to Kirkintilloch, a distance of 6¾ miles, in 103 minutes. But even Dragons could not long contend against the fire-breathing monsters that were overrunning the country, and in 1832 it is chronicled that most of the work is already done by two locomotives. As an instance of the consequent reduction of rates of carriage, it is added that, during the construction of the line, 6s. 11d. per ton was asked for the carriage of rails up from Kirkintilloch to Gargill; it can now be done for 9d. A second result is given in these words:—"The coal on one property previous to the commencement of the railway was offered at a rent of £30 a year and refused, and now the proprietor is obtaining £200 a year for it, and even this sum is expected soon to be doubled. The ironstone on another property was offered previous to the commencement of the railway for £100; it was afterwards sold for £500, and was thought a cheap bargain." One is glad to know that the railway company had some share in the prosperity which their enterprise had created. As early as 1828 they were getting 6 per cent. for their money, and their stock was at a premium of 50 per cent.

In May, 1826, a month or two before the Monkland and Kirkintilloch was opened for traffic, a new Act was obtained for the construction of a subsidiary railway, or, to speak more accurately, of a series of three branches, with a total length of 5¾ miles, to act as feeders of the main line. This new undertaking was known as the Ballochney.

The capital was fixed at the very precise figure of £18,491 19s., the exact amount of the engineers' estimate; and to the credit of the engineers be it that the line was opened for traffic with £200 of the capital unexpended. The Monkland and Kirkintilloch had traversed a tolerably level country; but the new road, which went up among the different collieries, passed through a more difficult district, so the tolls authorized were double those of the parent line, and amounted to 3*d.* per ton per mile for goods or minerals, with an additional 6*d.* per ton for each of the inclined planes over which they passed, and 4*d.* per mile for passengers. The method on which the line was worked is described in a contemporary account as borrowed from the Mawchunk Railway in America. A horse drew the loaded trucks along the level till they came to the top of the incline. Down the incline they would of course run by their own weight, so the horse was taken round to the tail of the train, where he became a passenger in a low wagon specially constructed for his accommodation, and refreshed himself with hay and water till his services were again called into requisition at the bottom.

The Ballochney Railway before long was paying 20 per cent., so in 1835 the Company obtained powers not only to make a new branch, but also to contribute half the capital to a more ambitious undertaking known as the Slamannan Railway, with a capital of no less than £65,769, which was to continue the railway system north-eastwards from the termination of the Ballochney, through Slamannan and Avonbridge to Causeway End, where it formed a connection with the Edinburgh and Glasgow Union Canal, and so gave a new and independent outlet to the Monkland Coalfield. Whatever was the reason, perhaps because at the outset it was weighted with so enormous a capital expenditure, the Slamannan was not like its predecessors a financial success. But 1835 is bringing us down to comparatively modern times, and this is not the place for a complete history of Scotch railways. So we must be content with just noting that in the year 1848 the three companies above named, the Monkland and Kirkintilloch, the Ballochney, and the Slamannan, amalgamated into one concern under the title of the Monkland Railways, that in 1865 the Monkland Railways were bought up by the Edinburgh and Glasgow Railway, which latter in its turn was absorbed the same year into the North British. We may notice too that, though for a mile or so northwards from the world-famous ironworks of Gartsherrie the Caledonian through trains to the North run over it under Parliamentary powers, the greater part of the original Monkland and Kirkintilloch line has long been closed to passenger traffic. It may be added further that, an outlet to a canal having ceased to be of any practical value, the old railways have been continued onward, the Monkland and Kirkintilloch to the shores of Loch Lomond, and the Slamannan to the port of Bo'ness [*i.e.*, Borrowstoneness] on the Firth of Forth.

The North British is, after all, but an intruder in this part of Scotland. Its proper territory lies rather on the East than on the West coast. The leading Glasgow railway is and has been from the first the Caledonian Company. And the line next in order of seniority to the Monkland and Kirkintilloch, the Garnkirk Railway, which obtained its Act in 1826, may fairly be looked upon as the nucleus of the Caledonian. Chronologically speaking, the gap between 1824 and 1826 is narrow enough, but the development of the railway idea in the interval is remarkable. The elder line was only intended to supplement water-carriage; the younger, which for practical purposes may be described as following throughout the course of the Monkland Canal, boldly challenged competition with it. And the challenge was not delivered without good reason. Glasgow had grown in the half-century since Watt's survey. The city gasworks alone were using, says a contemporary account, hard by 16,000 tons of coal per annum. Thirty thousand more were required by the chemical works at St. Rollox, then and now "perhaps the most extensive," as their chimney is probably among the highest, and certainly among the most odoriferous, "in the world." And the St. Rollox works adjoined the new Garnkirk terminus. Here the railway had a great advantage over the canal in its complete arrangements for rapid delivery. The trucks, we are told, ran in on a high level into the depôt; the body was tipped up at one end with the aid of a *dum-craft*, and the coal fell through trap-doors in the iron floor into carts which were in waiting beneath. The railway was opened in 1831, when amidst a scene of great public rejoicing the first train was drawn along the line by the " George Stephenson " engine, whose driver was none other than George Stephenson himself. The cost of the carriage of coal from the Monkland field to Glasgow fell within a short period from 3s. 6d. to 1s. 3d. per ton.

But great though the benefit might be which they had conferred on the citizens of Glasgow, the Garnkirk Company were not over prosperous themselves. On their 8¼ miles of line they had expended the enormous sum, as it was then considered, of over £12,000 a mile. They found it necessary therefore to exert their utmost efforts to augment their receipts. In the report for 1835 the directors, or rather the committee, to call them by the name in use at the time, confess to a " material increase of expenditure" in the item of advertising and printing. The amount for the year was £57 6s. 11d. "The reason is," they say, "that perseverance in frequently advertising the passenger carriages by newspaper notices and otherwise is found to promote an increase of trade amply justifying the expense so incurred." Here is an extract from the diary of the late Mr. Walter Linn, one of the too many officials of the original railways who have dropped off within the last few years, showing what we may fairly take as a specimen of the great results of the Company's lavish expenditure.

"*October* 23rd, 1834.—General Fast Day in Glasgow. A great crowd of people about the depôt all day; many passengers went up the railway.

1st train half-past 7 . .	6 coaches and 3 iron-wagons full.
11 o'clock . .	10 ditto and 8 ditto.
12 o'clock . .	19 coal-wagons full.
2 o'clock . .	9 coaches and 8 iron-wagons.
3 o'clock . .	4 coaches full.
5 o'clock . .	3 ditto.

"Everything moved on with the greatest regularity; not the least delay, nor did any accident take place, and not so much as one wagon went off the rails. We had about 1250 passengers out, and the whole of that number returned. Collected £60 1s. 6d." "Collected" is evidently the right word to use, for it was only in March, 1837, so

Mr. Linn records, that after a consultation with Mr. King, the secretary, he adopted the plan of supplying passengers with tickets before starting, and opened a booking-office for the purpose at St. Rollox.

In the same report the committee strikes out another idea. "It is intended," they say, "with the co-operation of the Monkland and Kirkintilloch and Ballochney Railway Companies, to add to the passenger trade the conveyance of goods and parcels between Glasgow and Airdrie. This branch of business may be ultimately let, perhaps, but in the first instance the Company will likely require to start it, or at least provide the necessary carriages and places for receiving and securing the goods. The shop in Glasford Street, occupied by the Company this season, was procured chiefly with a view to this trade; but the delay in proceeding with the requisite accommodation near Airdrie, for which this Company were dependent on another, has prevented it being yet applied to that purpose. Keeping open this shop in town has, however, been found of very considerable advantage to the passenger trade."

This proposal to let the conveyance of parcels and goods is worth notice as one instance of the fact—which cannot be too distinctly grasped by any one who wishes to understand not the ancient history of our railways merely, but also the

Growth of Passenger Traffic.

bearings of the very modern question of railway rates—that the original conception of a railway company was not that of a carrier at all, but simply of a company owning a road and charging a certain toll for the use of it. To quote one instance among a thousand. In 1837, several years after haulage by horses had disappeared from the line, and when therefore it is evident that the carriage of passengers must have become a monopoly of the Company, who alone possessed locomotives, the committee enter their passenger receipts under two heads. £1543 15s. is credited under the head of tolls, while a further sum of £1017 5s. is set down as received for haulage. The committee, by the way, were evidently very particular in keeping their accounts. A brick shed had to be repaired, and of the cost, £6 14s. 5½d. was allowed to be charged to capital, but the remaining 6s. was debited to the current year's revenue. Similarly some improvements in the Gartsherrie Inn were divided between two accounts, capital, £2 13s.; revenue, £1 18s. 3d. On the whole, the Garnkirk proprietors had reasons to be satisfied with the result of their attention to the passenger traffic. In the five years after the opening of the line the tonnage of minerals carried had only risen from 114,000 to 140,000. In the same period a steady and continuous increase had raised the number of passengers from 62,000 to 145,000.

We have almost forgotten the fact now-a-days, but railways in their early days had to compete for passenger traffic with something besides stage coaches. "Railroads, except in very peculiar circumstances, are behind the age," says in 1831 the author of a pamphlet written to prove the absurdity of building one between Edinburgh and Glasgow. He adds that the future is on the side not of cumbrous locomotives with their long lumbering trains, but of steam road-carriages, " of which a great many are already required by coach proprietors, carriers of merchandize, and others for their use on the public roads." This gentleman may be hardly an impartial witness, but it is at least certain that Mr. Scott Russell—afterwards the builder of the Great Eastern—established in 1834 "a line of steam coaches between Glasgow and Paisley, as the regular mode of conveyance. These ran for many months with the greatest regularity and success, and the trip, a distance of $7\frac{1}{2}$ miles, was run in 45 minutes. An accident caused by the breaking of a wheel which happened to one of the carriages being unfortunately attended with fatal results, caused the Court of Session to interdict the whole set of carriages from running."*

---

* The accident alluded to was nothing less than the bursting of the steam-coach boiler. These steam-coaches escaped the payment of tolls, which were by Act of Parliament authorized to be levied upon all vehicles " drawn by one or more

But steam road-carriages were not the only competitors. The track-boats on the canals must have been an almost equally speedy, and certainly a considerably safer mode of conveyance than the early railways. In a prospectus issued in 1836 for a much-planned but never-executed Garnkirk and Falkirk Junction Railway, it is stated that the passengers by canal between Falkirk and Glasgow amounted to 300,000 per annum, and though the distance cannot have been much under 30 miles, it is added that the journey was performed in 3 hours. Even the heavy barges with a load of 40 tons covered the 56 miles from end to end in 18 hours. On the Ardrossan Canal, says the same authority, one horse drew 60 passengers 8 miles, from Glasgow to Paisley in three-quarters of an hour, returning to Glasgow in the afternoon at the same pace. From Glasgow to Johnstone, 4 miles further, the time was an hour and half. From Liverpool to Sankey, on the road to Manchester—to quote a parallel English

---

horses, mules, &c." They were consequently the object of the fiercest hostility of the road trustees; and when the accident took place, owing to a wheel breaking on a newly-metalled portion of the road, it was openly asserted that the metal had been laid down extra thick with the object of disabling the new-fangled coach. Indeed, a very strongly-worded letter from the clerk to the trust, which had appeared in the newspapers only a few days before, was believed to point to an intention on the part of the trustees to pursue some such policy.

instance—the speed was 10 miles an hour. It is an interesting proof of the early adoption of the very low fares, which have long been one of the mosts creditable features of the traffic down the river from Glasgow, to learn that while the fares to Sankey were 3s. 6d. and 2s. 6d. those to Johnstone only one mile less distance, were 1s. and 9d.

The mention of the Ardrossan Canal brings us naturally to the third and last of the great railways of Scotland, the Glasgow and South-Western, of which this undertaking may be considered to be in some sort the nucleus. Let it be said, to start with, that the title is a somewhat ridiculous misnomer, for the Canal never got within 20 miles of Ardrossan. The full style and title was "The Glasgow, Paisley, and Ardrossan Canal," and its inception dates from 1804, in which year the then Lord Eglinton formed a company, and obtained an Act for its construction, with the evident intention of making Ardrossan, a place with great natural advantages, the outport for the rapidly growing trade of Glasgow. But fast as the trade grew, the faster the energy of the citizens worked to improve the navigation of the Clyde ; and the canal which commenced at "Tradestown, near Glasgow," now one of the busiest manufacturing quarters of the city, never got any further seawards than Johnstone. Here it stuck for over twenty years, till in 1837—the canal era having now given place to the railway age—its proprietors obtained leave to complete their route by the construction of a railway.

The waterway having begun to work downwards from the interior, it was only in the fitness of things that the railway should advance inwards from the sea-coast. And so it did; but it, too, stuck after it had got as far as Kilwinning, a distance of about 5 miles. It is true that the proprietors atoned for their failure to carry out their Act by the construction of two small colliery branches, for which they had no statutory powers whatever. The line was laid in the roughest and most haphazard fashion, but it served with considerable advantage, not only as a mineral line to Ardrossan Harbour, but also as a road for a one-horse omnibus, which ran backwards and forwards for the benefit of the population of Ardrossan and Kilwinning, as well as of the small towns of Stevenson and Saltcoats, which lie between them. In 1836 a company, which also deemed an Act of Parliament a superfluity, was projected with a capital of £5000 to " form an edge railway from the Dirrans branch of the Ardrossan and Johnstone railway to the town of Irvine, for the continued direct conveyance of Coals, Stones, Goods, Passengers, &c." Next year, the Glasgow, Paisley, Kilmarnock, and Ayr Railway, a company whose title is self-explanatory, obtained its Act; and in

1840 the 5 mile fragment of the Ardossan line took powers dissolving the Mezentian union with the moribund canal, and authorizing a junction with the new railway, in whose undertaking, now known as the Glasgow and South-Western, it has long ago been absorbed. It may here be appropriately added that the derelict canal was bought only a few years back by the South-Western Company, and filled up and converted into an alternative route to relieve the congestion on their main line into Glasgow.

It was stated at the beginning of this chapter that the earliest of the local trains preceded by fully twenty years the first of the through routes. But in tracing the history of a few of the more important of the former, we have now reached the point where the latter begins to appear upon the scene. The first proposal for a railway connecting England and Scotland was in the year 1832, for a line which has never been made from that day to this, and which—if railway prophecies were not proverbially even more fallacious than prophecies in general—one would be inclined to assert never would be.* The proposed route was from Newcastle,

---

* The ink that wrote this statement last July was scarcely dry when news was published of the proposed amalgamation of the North British and the Glasgow and South Western. This is not the place to discuss that question, but it may be pointed out that its natural effect would be to bring the

by Otterbourne, Jedburgh, and Melrose. Thence to Edinburgh it followed the present Waverley route by Galashiels, while a branch diverged up the Tweed and reached Glasgow by way of Peebles, Biggar, and the Clyde Valley. This route had one great and conspicuous advantage, it afforded equal accommodation to both Edinburgh and Glasgow. The East Coast road by Berwick, if it had been adopted as the only line between England and Scotland, would have placed Glasgow at an immense disadvantage. The western route by Dumfries and Kilmarnock would have been equally unsatisfactory to Edinburgh. And, as Mr. Gladstone told the House of Commons last year, even as late as 1842 "it was firmly believed to be absolutely impossible, that there should ever be more than one railway into Scotland."

Caledonian and the North Eastern into closer sympathy, and possibly to promote the development of a route not very dissimilar from that proposed in 1832. The Caledonian is already at Peebles in the upper valley of the Tweed; the North Eastern is at Kelso, some forty miles lower down on its course. The intervening stretch of railway is the property of the North British. If Parliament were to give running powers over it, either to the Caledonian, or to the North Eastern, or to both, a new direct route would be opened between Newcastle and Glasgow, free on the one hand from North British control through Edinburgh, and on the other avoiding the crowded traffic of the Newcastle and Carlisle road, the crush through Carlisle itself, and the formidable gradients of the Beattock "bank."

It is a commonplace of early English railway history to talk of the senseless opposition—where at least it was not a cloak for extortion—of the great landowners. Every one knows the story of the Duke of Cleveland's fox-covers which barred the progress of the Stockton and Darlington, and of the lords of Knowsley and Toxteth who turned aside the course of the Liverpool and Manchester. It was largely owing to the enlightened master of Althorp that Northampton was left for forty years stranded on one side of the great stream of traffic which swept through Blisworth. To the credit of the landlords of Scotland be it said, that the lairds of Dumfriesshire conceived and carried out the Caledonian Railway.

In 1836 the London and Birmingham, the Grand Junction, and the North Union were all fast approaching completion, and their united systems would convey passengers direct from London to Preston; so Joseph Locke was called in to survey a continuation northwards into Scotland. As far as the Scotch border, he recommended what is practically the existing West Coast line. Beyond that point, so he states in his report, he naturally first turned his attention to the direct mail-coach road, "laid out, I believe, by the late Mr. Telford." Along that route up to Beattock Bridge, near Moffat, he found everything tolerably favourable. But in the ten miles from Beattock Bridge to

Beattock Summit there would need to be a rise of "nearly 700 feet, which, supposing it to be uniform the whole way, would give an inclination of 1 in 75."

Ten miles of such a gradient the great engineer felt to be a hopeless impossibility. "Not wishing," he writes, "to recommend a line having such a plane as this, I was under the necessity of departing from the straight course." He turned aside reluctantly and advised a line up the gently sloping Nithsdale and over the Cumnock hills to Kilmarnock, and then on to Glasgow past Dalry and Beith and Paisley. The following year, as has been already mentioned, an Act was obtained for the construction of the portion of this route between Kilmarnock and Glasgow, and in the Mania year, 1846, leave was given to construct the remaining portion between Carlisle — or, more accurately, between Gretna, where it left the Caledonian — and Kilmarnock; but the promoters were no longer Joseph Locke's clients.

But let us return to his original report. This document was sent by Mr. Hope Johnstone, M.P., the largest proprietor in the Moffat district, to his agent, or factor, to use the Scotch expression, Mr. Charles Stewart. Mr. Stewart declined to abandon his hopes for an Annandale line. "As for *paying*," he writes, "I have no idea that it would do so immediately, but the country is now making such rapid strides in everything, that one would not despair of this, ultimately embracing, as it would do, a large share of the intercourse between England and Scotland." On the other hand he was entirely sure that "the passing of the railway up Annandale would be of incalculable importance to its prosperity ... would perhaps double the value of its productions in no distant time," and he accordingly determined that it was "only after every effort is made that the idea should be abandoned." He pointed out that, according to Telford's survey, the summit was 100 feet lower than Mr. Locke had made it; argued that a tunnel such as Mr. Locke had himself proposed at Shap did not "seem altogether out of the question;" suggested the use of stationary engines; anything rather than give up the line.

In the result a local committee was formed with Mr. Hope Johnstone at its head, subscriptions amounting to £150 were raised, and in the autumn of 1837 Mr. Locke, having got the Grand Junction open and off his hands, came down a second time to Scotland and resurveyed the line. Here is the pith of his observations on the crucial point, "the plane of the Evan," as he calls the ten miles of line, now-a-days (largely in consequence of the wonderful performances of Mr. Drummond's superb "No. 123" in the "Race to Edinburgh") known to railway men all over the world as the "Beattock

Bank." "The inclination," he writes, "is similar to those on the Liverpool and Manchester Railway, which are worked by assistant locomotive engines. Of the facilities of drawing up considerable weights at moderate speeds there is no doubt; in short the ascent involves nothing but more power and more time. In the descent, however, there is more danger, and this is a question of importance. Perfect machinery and perfect watchfulness on the part of the attendants leave no room for apprehension. A train of passengers on an inclined plane of 1 in 93 may be kept under perfect control by ordinary means. On the other hand a plane like this ought not to be adopted without sufficient reason. You cannot expect it to be so economically worked, nor so certain in its operation as a line of equal length that is free from such a plane."

Mr. Locke ended by giving the scheme a qualified approval, and suggested that, as the object was one of national importance, the Government should institute a thorough and minute inquiry into the competing proposals. This the Government did, and, as all the world knows, the commission reported in 1841 expressing "the preference they felt bound to give to the western route to Scotland by Lockerbie, under the supposition that at present one line of railway only can be formed from the South to Edinburgh and

Glasgow." Then followed a weary struggle of four more years. The Clydesdale landowners, who were as much concerned as their neighbours south of the watershed, were apathetic; Glasgow, interested in its Ayrshire line, was largely hostile; Edinburgh was desirous of an East Coast road all its own; everybody was waiting in the hope of Government assistance. Worse than all, a heavy cloud of trade depression overhung the country. But through it all the Annandale Committee held on. In 1844, by which time not only had trade much improved, but also some unknown genius had discovered a name suitable for the company which claimed to be the national line — the Caledonian Railway,—matters at length got to the point of issuing a prospectus. The capital asked for was £1,800,000. Next year, after a battle royal with the promoters of the Dumfries line, with eight counsel (among them Charles Austin) on the one side, and seven (among them Cockburn, Wrangham, and Hope Scott) on the other, the Caledonian Bill was passed through both Houses and received the Royal assent on the last day of July. The Annandale gentry had got their line, and their leader, Hope Johnstone, deservedly became the first chairman of the company. In the crash which followed the wild speculation of 1846, not a few of them, however, had reason to wish that the Evan Water had really been the impassible barrier which Locke at first had fancied it.

The English railway system is the result of fully a generation's growth. But the Scotch system, in plan, if not always in actual execution, sprang fullgrown from the brain of the projectors of '46. For this difference various reasons may be assigned. Scotland waited much longer before it began to construct through routes, and so had a long leeway to make up. Then again the physical geography of the country fixes the course of railways much more precisely than is the case in most parts of England. For a third reason, Scotland is not rich enough to indulge on any large scale in the luxury of parallel routes such as are found in England. Those who know the railway geography of Scotland to-day will appreciate from the perusal of the following list of Acts of Parliament passed in the Session 9 & 10 Victoria, for railways either originally constructed or since acquired by the Caledonian, how little, as far as this one railway at least is concerned, the projectors of 1846 left over for their successors.

The Scottish Midland Junction Railway Branches Act, 1846.
The Arbroath and Forfar Railway Act, 1846.
The General Terminus and Glasgow Harbour Railway Act, 1846.
The Dundee and Arbroath Railway (Extension) Act, 1846.
An Act to enable the Glasgow, Paisley, and Greenock

Railway Company to make a Branch Railway to the River and Firth of Clyde at or near Greenock, and a Pier or Wharf in connection therewith, 3rd July, 1846.

The Glasgow, Barrhead, and Neilston Direct Railways (Branches to Thornliebank and Househill) Act, 1846.

The Scottish Central Railway (Alloa Branch) Act, 1846.

The Scottish Central Railway (Denny Branch) Act, 1846.

An Act to enable the Glasgow, Paisley, and Greenock Railway Company to make a Branch Railway to the Polloc and Govan Railway, and to amend the Acts relating to the said Railway, 16th July, 1846.

The Scottish Central Railway (Perth Termini and Stations) Act, 1846.

The Scottish Central Railway (Crieff Branch) Act, 1846.

The Wishaw and Coltness Railway (Cleland Extension) Act, 1846.

The Glasgow Southern Terminal Railway Act, 1846.

The Dundee and Perth Railway Amendment Act, 1846.

The Caledonian Railway (Glasgow, Garnkirk, and Coatbridge Branch) Act, 1846.

The Caledonian Railway Carlisle Deviation Act, 1846.

The Caledonian Railway Glasgow Termini and Branches Act, 1846.

The Caledonian Railway (Glasgow, Garnkirk, and Coatbridge Railway Purchase) Act, 1864.

The Glasgow, Garnkirk, and Coatbridge Railway Extension Act, 1846.

The Caledonian, Polloc, and Govan and Clydesdale Junction Railways Amalgamation Act, 1846.

The Caledonian Railway (Clydesdale Junction Railway Deviations) Act, 1846.

At the first statutory meeting of the Caledonian, the chairman placed before the shareholders a summary of their position. They had got their Act for a line northwards from Carlisle, with branches to Edinburgh, to Glasgow, and to Castlecary for the North. Their access to Glasgow was already secured by agreement with the Garnkirk line. The Clydesdale Junction, which had been sanctioned that same session, would give them a connection to Paisley, to Greenock, and to Ayrshire. Northwards from Castlecary, the allied Scottish Central would carry them on to Perth, where the Scottish Midland, and then the Aberdeen Line would form the last links in the chain which stretched away to the metropolis of the North. "Companies with ample subscribed capitals and 10 per cent. deposited had been formed for extending the Caledonian system into every part of Scotland." Next year would see introduced bills for the following :—

1. The Caledonian Extension, from Lanark westward to Ayr, eastward to join the North-Eastern line at Kelso.
2. The Caledonian and Ayrshire Junction, to connect Kilmarnock with Railway No. 1, and thereby form a through route from Kilmarnock to Carlisle.
3. The British and Irish Union from Dumfries to Portpatrick.
4. The Caledonian and Dumbarton Junction, joining the Glasgow and Garnkirk line to Dumbarton, with possibly a further extension to the West Highlands.
5. A line from Perth to Inverness.
6A. Branches of the Scottish Central to Alloa and Crieff.
6B. Private lines to Tillicoultry and Dumblane.

A glance at a railway map will show that almost every one of these lines has now been carried out. Their course, however, was not always so smooth as Mr. Hope Johnstone fancied it about to be. They have not all been executed in the Caledonian interest, nor has their result been to secure to that company the impregnable position which the sanguine spirits in 1845 imagined themselves on the eve of securing. But though the hopes of 1845 were doomed to disappointment, the Scottish people can at least claim that, as they had been among the first to appreciate the value of railways for local traffic, so now they were among the first, if not indeed actually the first, to draw out on a large scale and in bold outline, a comprehensive scheme of railways in their newer development as the grand highways of national and international communication. In subsequent chapters we shall see that the modern performances of the Scottish lines are not all unworthy of their early promise.

II. THE OUTLOOK FOR THE FUTURE.

WE saw in the last chapter that universal and ubiquitous competition was the leading characteristic of the Scottish railway system. We saw too that the earliest lines were built without any thought of such conditions, merely for local traffic; that, for instance, in the immediate neighbourhood of Glasgow, there were, on the north side of the Clyde, alone, six independent companies; and that when, some twenty years later, the idea of through traffic first emerged, even then the railway magnates of the day contemplated nothing more than a series of allied companies forming separate links in a continuous chain; and that, accordingly, to take one example, the main high road from Carlisle to Aberdeen was divided into Caledonian, Scottish Central, Scottish Midland, and Aberdeen Line territory. Similarly it might have been shown that what is now the North British began—even confining ourselves to its main lines—as half-a-dozen separate companies. The Edinburgh and Berwick needed the alliance of the Edinburgh and Glasgow to bring it on to the west; that of the Edinburgh, Perth, and Dundee, to give it access to the north; while the Waverley route between Edinburgh and Carlisle was originally two separate systems, which met at Hawick. The Great North of Scotland is the result of almost as many amalgamations as it to-day has branches; while the Highland has absorbed the Inverness and Ross-shire, the Sutherland, the Duke of Sutherland's, and the Sutherland and Caithness, into a single company, which, if not in capital and importance, in length of main line at least, is the equal of the Midland, the superior of the North-Western, and the inferior of the Great Western Railway alone.

For practical purposes in all Scotland to-day there are only five companies. Four of them have been mentioned above; the fifth is the Glasgow and South-Western Railway. There is indeed a sixth, the City of Glasgow Union Company. But though it is known to the Stock Exchange as possessing a capital of £1,500,000 sterling, and to engineers as having a mileage of $6\tfrac{3}{4}$ miles to be maintained, *Bradshaw* is ignorant of it, for it does not own a single engine or a single carriage, and has never yet run a train of its own. It is really a short line round the south and south-east of Glasgow, uniting the North British and South-

Earthen Pots and Brazen Vessels. 41

Western systems, and worked entirely by those two companies. *Bradshaw*, however, does know of yet another company, the Ayrshire and Wigtownshire, the possessor—it cannot be said the happy possessor—of some thirty miles of single line across the barren South Ayrshire moors. But of this little line, which till recently was worked by the South-Western, more anon. It deserves notice, not only as an almost unique instance of a semi-absorbed undertaking escaping final deglutition,* but also for the pluck and energy with which it is at present struggling against an unkind fate.

Meanwhile let us admit that the existence of —with this exception—but five railways in all Scotland, the smallest of them with over 300 miles of line, is a testimony to the business-like capacity of the Scottish mind. From the Humber to the shores of Cardigan Bay, and from Yarmouth beach to the bed of the Mersey, England is strewn with the wrecks of the luckless little companies which—oblivious of the old adage as to the fate of earthen pots which swim down the stream alongside of brazen vessels—have been shattered to pieces in the vain attempt to compete with the

* The Neath and Brecon, whose lease to the Midland expired last summer, and which is now being fattened by Sir Edward Watkin as the prize lamb of his new Welsh Union flock, is a second.

overwhelming forces of their great rivals. Company after company in England has raised capital from confiding investors, on the faith of a prospectus showing that it could offer a route between A. and B. shorter by so many miles than the existing roads. The statement may have been mathematically accurate, but was really beside the point, unless it could be supplemented by evidence to show that the traffic was likely to follow the shortest road.

Take a familiar instance. A new direct line from Reading to Bath would shorten the distance between Paddington and the West of England some 14 miles. A prospectus, which laid stress on this fact, and then went on to describe the vast volume of traffic that flows to and fro between London and Bristol, would have a very enticing appearance at first sight. But the question to ask of the promoters would be: "What reason have you to suppose that you will be able to divert the existing traffic? The Great Western road of course is longer, but it is all their own; it is their agents who canvass in Bristol, in Plymouth, and in London, for the traffic which will be loaded at either end into trucks which are theirs: why do you expect that they will suffer it to pass out of their own control in order to swell the receipts of a 'foreign' line? If you say that you will get your share of the traffic handed to the Great

Western by other companies, are you not equally mistaken? Will the North-Western, for example, care to secure the friendship, or fear to rouse the hostility of the Reading and Bath Direct? If they were to offend the Great Western, it might be a serious matter; tens of thousands of pounds' worth of traffic which that great company now hands to them, might in this case be diverted to the Midland or the Great Northern. What bribe have you to offer to induce the North-Western to run this risk?" To such a string of questions the most sanguine promoter would find it difficult to furnish a satisfactory answer.

The truth is that there are only two conditions under which a small railway company can be a success. Either it must have a sharply defined district of its own in which the traffic is wholly or mainly local. Examples of this may be found in lines such as the Metropolitan among passenger railways; the Taff Vale, the Rhymney, or the Furness, among mineral lines. Or, on the other hand, it must be the possessor of a necessary link in a through chain of communication. The Lancaster and Carlisle paid fat dividends for years before it was bought by the North-Western on terms that its shareholders should receive in perpetuity $4\frac{1}{4}$ per cent. beyond the North-Western dividend; the Salisbury and Yeovil was yet more profitable to the fortunate farmers who had money and faith at a time when these two valuable possessions were more than usually wanting to the South-Western directorate. But the Lancaster and Carlisle and the Salisbury and Yeovil have long since been bought up—high though their terms were—by the great lines in whose territory they formed an *enclave*, and their day returns not. The primary lines of communication have all long since been formed, and the investing public seem at length to have begun to apprehend the fact that, where it is a question of supplying what might be termed secondary communications, the natural authority to supply them is the company whose system they lie in with. If it can construct the new line with a fair chance of profit, it is not likely to hold its hand; if the company itself cannot make the new venture pay, still less can outsiders.

Of railways of the Reading and Bath Direct order Scotland has none; with the natural result that there is hardly any—among independent companies not a single pound's worth of railway capital in all Scotland receiving no dividend. On the other hand, competition is too severe to make it possible for any railway capital to earn dividends, not merely such as are paid by the Taff Vale or the Rhymney, but even by the rank and file of the great through lines of England. When it comes to spending between four and five millions sterling—as is being done by the companies which are responsible for the Forth Bridge and its new approaches — in order to get a somewhat larger share of the through traffic to Aberdeen and the Highlands, it can hardly be expected that even the most skilful and economical of managers will obtain any very magnificent dividend. Indeed there are those who think that the scramble for traffic, which next year must, it is supposed, witness, is by no means likely to add to the value of Scottish railway securities.

Far be it from me to attempt to describe the great Forth Bridge. It has been described too often, and the literature of the subject, what with popular articles, and papers in the Proceedings of scientific societies, not only English but foreign, has already grown to alarming dimensions. Besides, when Mr. Baker himself has given more than one account of the wonderful structure which his engineering genius planned, and his patience, aided by the mechanical genius of Mr. Arrol, has now executed, it is as well for outsiders to leave him to speak. Let me here merely jot down one or two personal impressions. For one thing I must confess to feeling that a close view of the bridge is somewhat disappointing. Its vastness is so complete and symmetrical throughout that one fails to grasp it. Even the *Devastation*, as she lies moored close to the Inchgarvie pier, scarcely helps to furnish an adequate measuring-staff. The great ship seems dwarfed to a cock-boat and leaves the bridge no larger than before. The best idea of the size of the structure is obtained from a considerable distance. Seen from the train, as it glides down the slopes of the Pentlands into Princes Street Station, or from near Ratho on the Edinburgh and Glasgow line, or again from the deck of the ferry steamer, as she crosses the Forth between Granton and Burntisland, the great steel towers appear to soar aloft far above the tops of the not inconsiderable hills by which they are surrounded. Only once did the size of the bridge as a whole—there is no question that the size of the individual members is ample enough — impress itself forcibly on my eye. Coming out of the Queensferry Station, the whole length of the structure is full in view. My companion and myself stopped and questioned why no one was visible, and what was the reason that work had been suspended. As we got nearer, we found that everything was in full swing, workmen were clustered thick as flies all along the extremities of the cantilevers, but the flies were so small that they had been invisible.

When trains come to pass over the bridge, they will afford a convenient means of comparative measurement. Meanwhile there is nothing more instructive than a study of a large-sized model which has been erected in the pattern-shop in the

Queensferry yard. The girders that carry the rails are there seen to bear about the same relation to the cantilevers which carry the weight of the structure itself that a straw bears to a stout walking-stick. A locomotive is not a small object when viewed under ordinary conditions ; but a locomotive, modelled to scale, and shown crossing the bridge, produces much the same impression as a child's regiment of tin soldiers when marshalled on the nursery floor. On the same model is shown also an ingenious device to allow for the adjustment of the rails as the bridge expands or contracts with the changes of temperature. At certain intervals the rails, instead of being cut off square at the ends and fastened to each other by fish-plates in the ordinary fashion, are gradually tapered to a fine point, and overlap each other for several feet, the length of the over-lap being greater or less according to the rise or fall of the thermometer.

Now that the bridge is completed, its peculiarity of construction is hardly so conspicuous as it was at an earlier period. A year or so back no one who looked at the three great piers towering up, 360 feet in sheer height above the sea, and a third of a mile apart from each other, and just beginning to reach out their huge arms on either side, could possibly have fancied that what he saw was an ordinary bridge, dependent for its support on the principle of the arch. But now that the long arms stretching out from either shore have met the yet longer arms extended to meet them from Inchgarvie in mid stream, at first sight the idea of the arch might naturally be suggested. For all that, of course, the Forth Bridge cantilevers have nothing in common with the ordinary arch. A cantilever is simply a bracket, and the principle of the bridge is merely that three huge towers, each the height of the dome of St. Paul's, have brackets over an eighth of a mile in length, projecting out from them on either side. The brackets are pairs of steel tubes, big enough for a coach and horses to drive through, rising from the base of the piers, meeting at their further end the horizontal girders along which the railway runs, and supported at the same point by equally huge steel bands stretching downwards from the top of the piers. Engineers describe the tubes as compression members, and the bands as tension members; in plain English the tubes are props to support from beneath, and the bands are strings to hold up from above, the arms which are extended out horizontally from the centre. Indeed, Mr. Baker has given a graphic illustration of the design of the bridge, by photographing a living model, in which the piers are men seated on chairs, and stretching out their arms to grasp with either hand one end of a stick, which is attached at the other end to the seat of the chair.

One of the most difficult parts of the whole

problem was that which was dealt with after the cantilevers were finished. At the shore end on either side the Fife and Queensferry cantilevers meet the viaducts built out to join them from the land, to the outermost piers of which they are not only held down by enormous weights, but are also fastened by bolts, not however rigidly, but with freedom to move backwards and forwards on rollers, so as to allow for expansion and contraction with the varying temperature. But the cantilevers which balance them on the sides turned towards the stream fall short by more than 100 yards of meeting the pair of cantilevers stretching out from the central or Inchgarvie pier. How then were these two gaps—each twice the width of the widest arch of Blackfriars Bridge—to be bridged? Who was to lay, so to speak, the two planks across at a height of 164 feet above the flowing tide beneath? We call them planks, for so in effect they are; but the planks are steel girders, each 50 feet in depth from top to bottom.

The process adopted was somewhat as follows. Let us confine ourselves to one girder only, for they were both constructed in the same fashion. The girder was built up in two pieces, which were carried forward to meet one another in the middle. Till they met, they were rigidly connected, by ties at the top and supports at the bottom, on to the cantilevers of which for the moment they formed a part.

And so the building forward went on, till the two halves got within 4 inches of one another. Then the opportunity was carefully watched, as the structure lengthened or contracted with the change of temperature. As soon as they had approached as near to one another as they seemed likely to come, the two ends of the bottom booms were temporarily tied together, the string taking the form of ten plates of steel, $\frac{7}{8}$ of an inch thick, each plate 10 feet long and 8 inches wide. Next the top members of the girder had to be joined up, and when that too was completed, it was time for the temporary fastenings to be removed, and for the entire girder to be allowed to drop into its permanent resting-place on rollers at the ends of the two cantilevers. The engineers had calculated that, in order to prevent the completed girder from sagging, the top booms would have to be joined up at a temperature 14° lower than that prevailing when the bottom members were closed. But owing to the extraordinary mildness of the season, it was found impossible to secure such a range of temperature, so hydraulic presses, with a force of 400 tons, equivalent to a variation of some 6°, had to be called into action to aid the natural expansion and contraction of the steel.

To any one who has seen the present structure, which is estimated to have cost £3,201,617 8s. 11d. sterling, it is not a little surprising to find that, more than seventy years back, bridging the Forth at this point was looked upon as comparatively child's play. In a pamphlet published in Edinburgh in 1818, Mr. James Anderson, Civil Engineer and Land Surveyor, proposed the construction of a chain bridge, not of course for a railway, but for ordinary cart and carriage traffic. At a height of 110 feet above high water, sufficient to "allow a vessel of 400 tons burden to pass under with her top-gallant mast standing," the cost would, he estimated, amount at the outside to £205,000. Mr. Anderson's project seems to have met with considerable support, though nothing was done towards carrying it into execution. But in the year 1865 a joint committee of the North British and Edinburgh and Glasgow companies, whose scheme, one may assume, had to run the gauntlet of the criticism of Parliamentary Committees, obtained an Act authorizing the construction, not only of a bridge 2 miles in length, but also of 8 miles of approach line, for the very moderate outlay of £650,000.

This second scheme vanished presumably in the commercial crisis of the following year. But in 1873 it was revived, an Act obtained, and a company incorporated, with power to make the bridge, and to connect it on the north side with the existing railways by new lines to Dunfermline and to Burntisland. The capital was fixed at £1,250,000 shares and £416,666 debentures. The engineer was Mr..

E 2

afterwards Sir Thomas, Bouch, and the design was for a suspension bridge. But sufficient money was not forthcoming; so in 1878 the great railway companies came forward and guaranteed a net income of £35,000 a year, the North British, the Midland, and the two East Coast companies jointly, each assuming the responsibility for one third of the amount. Before anything was done, down went the Tay Bridge and with it the reputation of Sir Thomas Bouch and the confidence of the public in great suspension bridges.

After another interval, and the promotion, in 1881, of an Abandonment Bill, the Midland in 1882 took the lead in the course which finally secured the erection of the bridge. It induced its partners to increase their guarantees, and to make themselves responsible for 4 per cent. interest on the whole of the Forth Bridge, as well as for the cost of maintenance, repair, and management. Of course the money was at once found without difficulty, Mr. Baker's design for a cantilever bridge was adopted. Mr. Arrol became the contractor, and the work proceeded, which on March 4th, 1890, is to be crowned by a ceremonial opening by the Prince of Wales.

What maintenance and repair will cost, no one yet knows, but for mere interest the Midland will have in future to find £40,000 per annum, the North British £37,000, and the East Coast companies £46,000 between them. The gradual growth of the estimated and still more of the actual cost from the original £205,000 is interesting as showing how thoroughly the Tay Bridge disaster has taught engineers the lesson that, with structures of this magnitude, provision against the weight of the load is a small matter compared with precautions against stress of wind. The new Tay Bridge is 2 miles in length, and spans not a deep gorge like that at Queensferry, but a wide open valley and a shallow stream, with foothold for innumerable close-ranked piers, and yet it has cost over £650,000, without leaving any margin for approach lines.

And in the case of the Forth Bridge scheme, the cost of the approach lines, which, except as to the 2⅞ miles immediately adjoining the bridge, has to be borne by the North British unaided, will certainly be well over a million sterling. First of all, a new direct road has to be made from Edinburgh, or at least from Corstorphine, on the south east, and from Winchburgh, that is from Glasgow, on the south west, to the bridge, as the present road goes round two sides of a triangle. Then on the Fife shore the existing line is down 200 feet below the rail-level of the bridge, and to effect a junction it is necessary to go back a long way and execute very heavy rock cuttings and raise vast embankments. Then again not only are the Fife railways for the most part single line, but they also run as a general rule east and west, following both the contour of the country and what has hitherto been the natural course of its communications. To form, therefore, a direct through express route to Perth, corners have to be cut off here, there, and everywhere, and of course single line has in each case to be doubled. Finally, when the route gets within about a dozen miles of Perth, an entirely new line has to be constructed to carry it through Glenfarg.

That Glenfarg is not exactly the place which any engineer would choose of his own free will for a railway is sufficiently proved by the fact that, though it was the mail-coach route in the old days from Edinburgh to Perth, no attempt has hitherto been made to run a railway through it. The new line strikes the glen at Damhead, 3 miles north of its junction with the existing line at Mawcarse, and for these 3 miles the country is easy enough. But from Damhead onwards is a narrow glen where stream and coach road jostle one another for lack of space. To find room for the railway by their side, the road is almost re-made, and the stream has more than once to be bridled and trained to run in a new and less rugged bed. Mile after mile, the railway descends with a gradient of 1 in $74\frac{1}{4}$; but the Farg falls faster yet, so in the lower portion of its course the line is carried high above it in cuttings half-way up the precipitous hills which form its banks. Twice over it avoids a sweep of the river by a plunge into a tunnel pierced through solid rock. Emerging from the second plunge, the scenery changes with startling abruptness from a Highland glen to the rolling slopes of Strath Tay, along which the railway descends directly upon Bridge-of-Earn, there to form a junction with the existing line from the Fife coast to Perth.

Glenfarg is likely in the summer of 1890 to see some remarkable feats of speed, but it will hardly see anything to beat in its own line the record of Captain Barclay's famous "Defiance" coach along the same road. The "Defiance," with her 15 passengers, to say nothing of guard, coachman and luggage, was timed to cover the 129¾ miles from the Waterloo Hotel in Edinburgh to Aberdeen in 12 hours 10 minutes, including the crossing at Queensferry and 30 minutes' stoppages. Down Glenfarg, the last 8½ miles into Perth was done in 40 minutes.

Perth, however, is not the only objective point for which the North British is making. It has at present much the shortest road, both in time and mileage, from Edinburgh and the South to Dundee, and *via* Dundee to Montrose and Aberdeen. But its road includes a 5 miles' steamboat journey across the Forth from Granton to Burntisland, and when the east wind is blowing in Edinburgh, as it usually is, the would-be passenger not unnaturally puts to himself the question which was asked of the lovely Rosabelle, "Why cross the stormy Firth to-day?"

and having put it, takes a ticket for the longer but all-rail route of the Caledonian Company. And if this interruption of the journey is bad for passenger traffic, still more is it so for goods, and especially for the immense traffic in perishables, such as fish and meat, which are sent from Aberdeen and Forfar to the markets of the south. When the connection now being formed from the Forth Bridge to the present Burntisland line is complete, the distance will be some 10 miles longer, but it will be by rail throughout, and will still remain shorter than that *viâ* the Caledonian line. And now let us see in brief summary what the North British and their allies will gain to compensate them for the expenditure of about four and a half millions sterling upon the complete scheme of which Forth Bridge is the central point. Let us put it in the form of a table.

From London to Perth :—
  By West Coast   is now 450 miles ; will be 450 miles.
  ,, Midland Route ,,   475½ ,,   ,, 455 ,,
  ,, East Coast   ,,   462 ,,   ,, 441½ ,,
i.e. East Coast was 12 miles worse, and will be 8½ miles better than West Coast.

From London to Aberdeen :—
  By West Coast   is now 540 miles ; will be 540 miles.
  ,, Midland Route ,,   565½ ,,   ,, 536½ ,,
  ,, East Coast   ,,   552 ,,   ,, 523 ,,
i.e. East Coast was 12 miles worse, and will be 17 miles better than West Coast.*

---

  * I have altered the figures in the above table more than once. They are probably not accurate even now, but the inaccuracy can only be trifling. As soon as the new lines are

"Magnificent, but not war!" one feels naturally tempted to exclaim, as one contemplates these figures, especially when one remembers what is likely to be the cost of the maintenance of the bridge, with its acres of exposed ironwork ready to absorb tons upon tons of paint, and to employ the labour of whole gangs of painters all the year round from January to December. And yet, though it is more than probable that the bridge would have never been built at all if the Companies concerned had realized at the outset how much it was to cost them, perhaps the croakers are wrong, and the wisdom of the undertaking may yet be justified. Certain it is, that the companies which have inherited the monumental lines, built regardless of expense by Stephenson or Brunel half a century back, have never had occasion to regret the outlay, and that many a company, whose roads date from the lean years which succeeded 1848, would give a good deal nowadays to secure that the work had not been done so cheaply in the

---

open for traffic we shall get official figures; but not till then. Meanwhile, it is worth mentioning, as a proof of the keenness of the competition, that my attention is called from the rival camp to the fact that the East Coast route is really 53 chains (⅔ of a mile) longer than it is commonly set down as being, because the official distances are taken (1) through the short loop at York instead of through the station, a difference of 37 chains, and (2) only to the junction outside Newcastle Station, a difference of twice 8 = 16 chains more.

first instance. Another thing is, I think, certain ; we have hardly yet begun to realise the dimensions to which passenger traffic may grow with another generation. Season-ticket traffic is still in its infancy. Holidays are becoming more and more common, and the number of those who can afford to travel on them is yearly becoming greater. If the working-classes, who are steadily cutting down the drink-bill, only come to expending half their economies in railway fares, this alone would suffice to pay handsome dividends on a whole series of Forth Bridges.

One thing is clear : the effect of the opening of the Forth Bridge will be felt right away to the extreme north of Scotland. The Highland express leaving King's Cross at 8 P.M. is in Edinburgh at 4.45 next morning. The relief train, which in the height of the August traffic leaves a quarter of an hour earlier, arrives at 4.23 A.M. This train therefore might easily be at Perth, only 48 miles further, by 5.30. Last year, *viâ* Larbert, it was seventy minutes later. The West Coast relief train which comes first was only due in at 6.35. But we are promised that in the future, whatever the East Coast does, that the West Coast will do also. So next summer, at least during the fortnight while these relief trains run, we may take it for granted that their passengers will be hurrying northward by 5.45, and that they will atone for the sin of rushing up the Pass of Killiecrankie in their sleeping-berths—for the sleeping-cars will evidently have to go beyond Perth in future—by appearing in Inverness in good time for a ten-o'clock breakfast. This is simple enough for the "grouse" fortnight; but what will happen during the rest of the year is by no means so self-evident. The Highland mail for eight months of the year probably takes half as many passengers *per diem* as in August it takes carriages, and would not be run as an express at all except for the very heavy Post Office subsidy. Now the special postal train does not leave Euston till 8.30 P.M., and is not due at Perth till 7.35 next morning. It is probably impossible for it to start any earlier, certainly quite impossible for it to start much sooner, for not only must it wait for the London letters, but also it works in close correspondence with the Irish mail, which leaves at 8.30, and runs almost alongside of it between Stafford and Crewe. Nor can the train, a pretty heavy one, be very much accelerated *en route*. To get it to Perth by 6.30 is the very utmost that the West Coast companies can possibly hope for. But something not much less than this they will be constrained to do. For the 8 o'clock out of King's Cross will be at Perth by 6, and if passengers for the Highland line are kept waiting too long, they will be apt to consider the possibility of going round the other way.

For it must always be remembered that the road through Glenfarg to Perth is henceforward not the only string to the East Coast bow. They are eight or ten miles nearer to Perth than the West Coast, but their advantage to Aberdeen will be just twice as great. Of this advantage the North British might be trusted to avail itself to the uttermost, were it only in order to make certain of securing the whole of the valuable traffic between Edinburgh, Dundee, and Aberdeen. But when there is a question in addition whether some of the English traffic, which at present goes through Blair Athole, might not be taken round *viâ* Aberdeen, there is still stronger reason. We shall probably not be far wrong if we say that by the East Coast Aberdeen will be brought within $11\frac{1}{2}$ hours of London; and once more, what the East Coast does, that the West Coast undertakes to do also. Will this make it possible for the old Aberdeen route to the north of Scotland to compete with the newer one by the Highland line? That the Great North of Scotland will do all in its power to secure this result, may be taken as certain, and if pluck and energy can secure it they are not likely to fail. To Inverness itself, even if they get their new independent line all the way, they can scarcely hope to obtain much of the traffic; but it may be otherwise with Keith, with Elgin, and the other places lying to the east of the

The Unique Railway Phenomenon. 61

Highland road. Then, moreover, when the new short line from Aviemore, of which more anon, is made, Forres and Nairn also will cease to be on the Highland main line, and accordingly the Great North may secure a share of their traffic also. As for places beyond Inverness, if the Great North gets its Bill, and if passengers will submit to the change into a ferry-steamer, it is possible that they may be reached almost as quick by the one line as by the other. But the problem in the North is all "ifs" at present.

"But why, in the name of fortune," one may fancy an English reader exclaiming, "take all this trouble and make all this fuss about the traffic to a petty country town like Inverness with a population of under 20,000 people, and to the even more insignificant places in its neighbourhood?" The question would be a very natural one, for certainly no one, unless he has seen Euston and King's Cross about 7.30 in the evening during the first week of August, or (still more remarkable) Perth about the same hour the following morning, can have any conception of the dimensions of the Highland traffic in the height of the season. Here is Mr. Foxwell's account ('Express Trains, English and Foreign,' p. 62), not one whit exaggerated :—

"In July and August the 7.50 A.M. train is the unique railway phenomenon. Passenger carriages, saloons, horse-boxes, and vans, concentrated at Perth from all parts of

England, are intermixed to make an irregular caravan. Engines are attached fore and aft, and the procession toils pluckily over the Grampians. Thus, on August 7, 1888, this train sailed out from Perth composed as follows :—

London & Brighton Co.'s horse-box.
London & Brighton Co.'s horse-box.
London & Brighton Co.'s carriage-van.
London & Brighton Co.'s horse-box.
North-Western, horse-box.
North-Eastern, ,,
North-Western, saloon.
 ,, horse-box.
Midland, saloon.
 ,, luggage-van.
 ,, carriage-truck.
 ,, horse-box.
North Western, horse-box.
North-British, luggage-van.
 ,, horse-box.
 ,, ,,
North British, horse-box.
East Coast, sleeping-car.
Great Northern, saloon.
West Coast, composite.
Midland, composite.
North-Western, luggage-van.
South-Western, horse-box.

West Coast, composite.
North-Western, horse-box.
 ,, meat-van.
Highland Railway, P. O. van.
 ,, ,, luggage-van.
Highland Railway, third-class passenger.
Highland Railway, first-class passenger.
Highland Railway, second-class passenger.
Highland Railway, third-class passenger.
Highland Railway, luggage-van.
Highland Railway, third-class passenger.
Highland Railway, first-class passenger.
Highland Railway, third-class passenger.
Highland Railway, guard's van.

9 Companies . 36 carriages

2 engines in front, 1 put on behind at Blair Athole."

The present writer was at Inverness on August 16th of that same year, when the fiercest rush of the traffic was already subsiding. The mail train, which starts for the north at 12.10 P.M., left with

20 carriages on, and hardly a vacant seat in any one of them: the up mail at 3 P.M. consisted of 22 coaches. And this is the normal state of things for a couple of months. When it is added that a very large proportion of this enormous traffic is first-class, and booked for hundreds of miles, with additional fares for sleeping-berths and saloons, or for excess luggage, it is sufficiently evident that, while it lasts, it must be splendidly profitable. No wonder the companies fight keenly for it.

Certainly the travelling public would have every reason to be grateful for anything that might divert some portion of the traffic that blocks Perth Station and its approaches every morning and evening in the month of August. The station cannot well be enlarged any more, for it is a Sabbath day's journey from one end of it to the other already. And in the hour between 6.35 and 7.35 A.M. there are poured into it from the south six or seven trains with a total length of fully half a mile, made up of every kind of vehicle, from horse-boxes and dog-carriages to sleeping-saloons and letter-tenders. How many possible permutations and combinations can be formed when three trains from Euston and two trains from King's Cross, with additions perhaps from Manchester and Liverpool, and from miscellaneous roadside stations, are rearranged so to form two trains for Inverness, a third for Aberdeen, and a fourth for

Dundee, it would need a mathematician to calculate. But lest he should think his task too simple, it may be added that each train must be marshalled in a particular order, as here a horse-box, and there a saloon, have got to be dropped at roadside stations all along the route. A similar state of affairs occurs in the evening, when the 6.41 from Dundee, the 6.45 and 7.5 from Aberdeen, and the 7 P.M. from the Highland, have all to be marshalled to form the 7.20 for Glasgow, the 7.30 West Coast, and the 7.35 for Edinburgh and London (both King's Cross and St. Pancras) each of these trains in all probability running in duplicate; while perhaps during the operation a couple of fish specials flit through on their way to England.

Nor have those responsible for the management of the station the advantage of exercising an undivided authority. Perth Station belongs, it is true, mainly to the Caledonian Company; but the Highland and the North British have also a share in the ownership, while no less than five other companies, the North-Western, the Great Northern, the North-Eastern, the Midland, and the Glasgow and South-Western, have, whenever they please, the right to run their own trains into it. One curious result of this diplomatic complication was seen the other day, when an assistant to the Perth station-master had to be appointed. The task of selection was assigned to the superintendents of the North-Western and the Great Northern, as representing the two chief rival influences, and they chose their man from the neutral territory of the Lancashire and Yorkshire, on the express ground that he was likely to exercise his authority with complete impartiality.

The passenger who is kept waiting at Perth must at least admit that there is not much fault to be found with the accommodation there provided for him. Even the very dogs are not forgotten, and after their hot night in the train, should enjoy their roomy kennels with fresh water and clean straw. For their masters there are comfortable dressing-rooms with baths all complete, while downstairs the breakfast, with its never-ending relays of fresh Tay salmon, can fairly challenge comparison with the famous *bouillabaisse* of the Marseilles *buffet*. If the rival companies, by the way, really do intend to run their passengers into Aberdeen for breakfast, they will certainly have to look after the refreshment arrangements at that station. Even at Mugby Junction itself they would have blushed to charge twopence for a penny bun, and threepence for a sandwich composed of equal parts of gristle, fat, and sawdust. But at Aberdeen they have no such scruples, being apparently under the impression that wine is not the only article in which old age may properly be paid for.

The complication of the relationships between

the different companies at Perth is only typical of that subsisting over a large part of Scotland. England has nothing to show at all equal to it, the nearest approach perhaps being on the lines to the east and south of Manchester. Everywhere two companies are to be found competing with one another for traffic, not by different routes, but over the same metals. For example, the Caledonian and the Glasgow and South-Western both use the same road for their Greenock trains as far down as Paisley. Carlisle Station is the joint property of the Caledonian and the North-Western; but the North-Eastern, the Midland, and the Maryport and Carlisle on the English side, and the North British and the South-Western on the Scottish side, have running powers not only into the station itself, but over a good many miles of the road outside it as well. In return, the North British is under statutory obligation to compete with itself by bringing the Caledonian trains from Larbert and the North on into its own Edinburgh station of Waverley. Or again, a branch has recently been constructed off the Glasgow, Barrhead, and Kilmarnock line, which the Caledonian owns jointly with the South-Western, and over it the Caledonian competes with the South-Western to Ardrossan and the watering-places on the Clyde. Or once more, the South-Western and the Midland, the Caledonian and the North-Western, unite in the joint ownership of the line which runs across Kirkcudbright and Wigtownshire from Castle Douglas to Stranraer, and send their combined trains over it. But the only access to it is along the South-Western metals from Dumfries to Castle Douglas.

These latter intricacies, however, are as nothing to those existing to the north of Edinburgh and Glasgow. Larbert, some eight or nine miles south of Stirling, occupies in railway diplomacy a position as important as that belonging to Luxemburg or Constantinople in European politics. Here from very early times the West Coast and Glasgow traffic of the Caledonian, the Glasgow traffic of the Edinburgh and Glasgow Company, and the East Coast traffic of the North British, all met, and the whole was taken on northward to Perth by the Scottish Central. In 1865 the North British proposed to amalgamate with the Edinburgh and Glasgow. But the Scottish people are disbelievers in railway monopolies, and were determined to keep open the door of free and unchecked competition, and the Select Committee gave full effect to their desire. Accordingly, in the Act of Parliament authorizing the union clauses were inserted by which all possible powers of through booking, running their own trains if desired, &c., were given to the Scottish Central Company, as well as to what are known as the East Coast Companies, that is to the Great Northern and the North-Eastern.

Then, the same year, the Scottish Central itself applied for leave to amalgamate with the Caledonian. It got its Act; and in the following session of 1866, a second Act authorized a further amalgamation with the Scottish North-Eastern, thus carrying on the Caledonian all the way to Aberdeen. Again the most stringent terms were insisted on. The North-Western and the Midland were given powers to run, not only northward to Aberdeen, but actually into the Caledonian terminus at Princes Street, Edinburgh, and at Buchanan Street, Glasgow.* The Glasgow and South-Western Company was treated with almost equal generosity. As for the traffic of the competing East Coast Companies, it was laid down in the Act, that it was to be treated by the amalgamated companies "as if it were their own proper traffic, or traffic which they were desirous of cultivating to the utmost." Yet more remarkable, it was provided that almost equal privileges must be conceded over any lines to the north of Larbert, which the Caledonian might construct at any future time. This last provision, inserted doubtless with the best intentions, has had one effect which its authors can scarcely have foreseen. For all practical purposes the Callander and Oban line is a part of the Caledonian. The larger part of

---

* This was, of course, long before the present Central Station was built, and when Buchanan Street was the chief Caledonian station in Glasgow.

its stock is held by the Caledonian Company, a good slice of the rest being held by the North-Western, and it is and always has been worked by the Caledonian. But, technically speaking, it is an independent company, and over it therefore the statutory rights of the North British over lines north of Larbert do not accrue.

There are not a few persons who think that the Caledonian might have been wiser if they had refused to accept their Amalgamation Acts at all on such onerous terms. For, when the Forth Bridge is opened, they will find themselves in a very peculiar position. The North British will have a route, both to Perth, and to Aberdeen *vid* Dundee and the Tay Bridge, of which it will have practically complete control. But the Caledonian route will still remain subject to all the existing obligations to accommodate North British traffic. No wonder that the North British star is somewhat in the ascendant just at present. Latterly it has succeeded to the position which was held by the Midland in the days of Sir James Allport. It seems to have taken Danton's words, "*De l'audace, de l'audace, et toujours de l'audace,*" as its motto, and so far with as much success as was attained by Danton's disciples. For it has by no means confined its attention to the Forth and Tay Bridges, and the east coast of Scotland. Its own proper exit from Glasgow was out to the high ground on the north-east; and when, some years back, it acquired possession of the line down the right bank of the Clyde to Dumbarton and Helensburgh, it was hampered in the user of it by the necessity of working round the northern outskirts of Glasgow from east to west.

Recently, mainly by the advice and assistance, it is understood, of the great firm of the Bairds of Gartsherrie, it has taken a new departure. It has constructed a railway, the "City and District," right under the heart of Glasgow. The line commences on the east side by a junction with the existing lines, passes under the terminus of the original Edinburgh and Glasgow Railway in Queen Street, and joins the Helensburgh line some miles out towards the west. With this one stone, and not a very expensive stone either, the North British has killed a whole covey of birds. It has secured a most convenient new road to the docks on the north bank of the Clyde. Secondly, it has obtained a very large urban passenger traffic, which formerly went by omnibus or tramcar—so large indeed that, though the line was primarily built as a goods road, goods have never yet been brought on to it. Thirdly, the new railway has enabled the company to try the experiment, which Sir Edward Watkin on the Metropolitan also appears to regard with favour, of combining urban with long-distance traffic. Trains run fast up to the outskirts of the city, from Edinburgh on the one side, and from Helensburgh on the other, and then stop at every station on the underground portion of the journey.

But the main interest of the "City and District" is to be found in its connection with the new West Highland route, for which Parliamentary sanction was obtained last session. It should be noticed that, just as the Callander and Oban is nominally independent of the Caledonian, so the new line is nominally independent of the North British. But as the North British is to work it, and as all the dividend it is likely to pay to start with will be derived from a North British guarantee, the outside public need hardly trouble themselves with the distinction. Starting from the Clyde, nearly opposite Greenock, the new railway will run north along the Gareloch and Loch Long to the head of Loch Lomond; then up Glen Falloch, till at Crianlarich, on the western slopes of Ben More, it strikes the Callander and Oban line, as it toils up the valley by which the Dochart runs down to the head of Loch Tay. Still northwards across the head-waters of the Tay, right through the desolate moor of Rannoch—the carriage of whose timber may be expected, so one enthusiastic witness declared, to furnish a handsome source of revenue to the company—and along Loch Treig till it reaches Glen Spean. Then due west till it strikes the banks of the Lochy and the Caledonian Canal, along which it bends round south-westwards, till it finally arrives at Fort William.

As originally presented to Parliament, the scheme provided for an extension to Roshven in Moidart, for the benefit of the fishermen and crofters of the western coast; but this portion of the undertaking was struck out in Committee in the House of Lords. But even so, the scheme as passed is large and far-reaching enough, and roused a strong though unsuccessful opposition on the part both of the Caledonian and the Highland Companies. As mentioned above, the new line cuts the Callander and Oban at right angles at Crianlarich, some forty miles from Oban. Now, there is a very considerable and a rapidly increasing traffic from Glasgow to Oban, and a line going straight up Loch Lomond is some seventeen miles shorter than a line running round by Larbert and Stirling. Naturally the Caledonian objected to the risk of seeing their traffic taken from them just as their line has begun to pay. They pointed out that the country northwards from Crianlarich could not furnish traffic enough to pay working expenses. If communication was wanted to the north of Oban, it should only be, they declared, along the coast. They would pledge themselves to make forthwith a coast-line from Oban, across Loch Etive and along the shores of Appin to

Ballachulish, where at least the slate quarries had attracted the nucleus of a population. But Parliament refused to listen.

The Highland Company had more than one ground of objection. Loch Treig, along which the new line is to pass, is only some dozen miles west of the Highland line, where it takes a great sweep to the westward by Dalnaspidal and Dalwhinnie in order to get over the Grampians through the Drumouchter Pass. And one main source of Highland revenue is the enormous sheep traffic from the moors of Perthshire and Inverness-shire, which it taps at this point. But this was comparatively a small matter. The apple of the Highland's eye is Inverness, and a railway at Fort William, or, what was worse, on the banks of the Caledonian Canal a dozen miles nearer than Fort William, is perilously close to Inverness itself. Where a canal could go, a railway could not find it difficult to follow. Moreover, the proposal of an extension to Roshven suggested only too clearly the possibility of a future competition with Strome Ferry, which even now is suffering from the rivalry of the much more distant port of Oban. But the diplomacy of the North British was equal to the occasion. By some means or other not easily intelligible to the outside observer, the opposition of the Highland Company was disarmed, the West Highland Act is now safely passed, and preliminary work on it has already been begun. As it has the support not only of the North British, but of the local landowners along the route, there can be no doubt whatever that its construction will be pushed steadily forward.

One thing is certain, that the position in which the Highland Company finds itself is no enviable one. If on the one side it is liable to be hard pressed by the opposition of the West Highland, on the other the Great North, a line which has enormously improved within the last few years, is, as has been said, doing its utmost to get access to Inverness and Dingwall. No amount of genius can extract much sustenance for railways any more than for man and beast from the barren hills of Perthshire or Inverness. The Highland must always mainly depend for a dividend upon its through traffic. And its through traffic it is forced to carry over a single-line route so tortuous that, though the total distance from Wick to Perth, as the crow flies, is only 125 miles, the railway is 305 miles in length. A year or two back, in order to keep out the Great North, it took powers for the construction of a new direct line from Aviemore to Inverness, cutting off the great elbow round by Forres and Nairn and so saving no less than 24 miles of distance. Having got its powers, it did nothing towards making the line. But when the Great North announced their intention to apply for powers to Inverness, the Highland dared not wait longer. It could never face a Parliamentary Committee and maintain that the existing facilities to Inverness were sufficient, when it had taken no steps to supply the additional accommodation whose necessity it had itself asserted only a few years before. So the board resigned itself to the inevitable, and last December contracts were invited for the construction of the new lines.

Small blame, however, to the Highland Company that it hesitated. If the opinion expressed the other day to the present writer by a very competent observer—not, it must be confessed, over-friendly to the Highland Company—may be trusted, the contruction of the new road will mean to them: in the first place, a capital expenditure of some hundreds of thousands of pounds; secondly, the cost of working some thirty additional miles; thirdly, no additional traffic whatever; and lastly, the reduction of the passenger fares by as many pence as the new road will be shorter in miles than the old.

The Forth Bridge and the new Highland schemes are, as has already been said, by no means the only, scarcely even the most important, signs that we are on the eve of great excitement in the railway world of Scotland. The proposal for an amalgamation of the North British and the Glasgow and South-Western fell upon the Stock

Exchanges last summer as a bolt from the blue. Nearly a quarter of a century has elapsed since the latter company tried and failed to secure an amalgamation, first with the Caledonian and then with the Midland. Sixteen years ago Parliament refused its sanction to the yet larger scheme for the union of the North-Western and the Lancashire and Yorkshire. And now the dawn of what seems likely to be a fresh era of railway prosperity is again giving rise to a series of similar proposals.

So far at least, if one may judge from the newspapers, the present scheme has this peculiarity, that it does not seem to have roused much outside opposition. The Midland and South-Western amalgamation fell through largely owing to the natural reluctance of the Scottish traders to have the management of their affairs removed from Scotland to Derby. The other two failed because they would have prevented a competition which it was thought desirable in the public interest to maintain in force. Neither of these objections can be urged against the present scheme. Both companies are purely Scottish, and their systems, which only meet at Glasgow and at Carlisle, nowhere compete with one another, except indeed—a big exception doubtless—for through traffic from England. It will perhaps be said that the North British has not as good a reputation for liberality to its customers as the

South-Western. But to this it is only fair to reply that the North British reputation was acquired in days when it was in a position of chronic impecuniosity, and that, now it has got into easier circumstances, it shows considerable improvement.

Anyway, public opinion seems ready to condone the North British sins, if it has any, and though it is understood that some of the leading traders in Glasgow are prepared to oppose, it is probable that the fight will be in the main an inter-railway one. But this limitation will not prevent it from becoming a battle royal. The three great Scottish companies, with their two thousand odd miles of line and their hundred millions of capital, are in it as principals. Then, of course, the Midland must support the amalgamation. The Glasgow and South-Western, whose board is presided over by the Midland chairman, has been a Midland dependency for twenty years past, and it is inconceivable that it could have thrown itself into the all-embracing arms of the North British if the Midland had desired to forbid the banns. Equally of course, the North-Western will support the Caledonian in opposition. The uncertain factor in the case is the attitude of the East Coast Companies, the North-Eastern and the Great-Northern. It is impossible to imagine that they will support the Bill; but will they oppose it, or will they simply remain neutral?

For my own part, I am convinced they are bound

to oppose it. Even the proverbial Englishman of the French story-books does not sell his wife quite for nothing, and the Midland is not surrendering to the North British its control of the South-Western without receiving a *quid pro quo* somewhere and somehow. One form which that *quid pro quo* might take can be easily seen. The London traffic with Glasgow, for instance, goes partly by West Coast, partly by Midland and Glasgow and South-Western, partly *viâ* Edinburgh and the East Coast. The North British, if it gets its Bill passed, will have no interest in sending anything by this third route. It will have an easier road and will get an equal share of the mileage rate if it sends *viâ* Carlisle, and once at Carlisle the Midland would naturally carry the traffic the rest of the distance. Exactly the same considerations apply to the traffic between Glasgow and Leeds. As for traffic from the north of Scotland, the East Coast companies are not likely, if they can help it, to find £50,000 a year to pay their share of the interest guaranteed for the Forth Bridge, and then to submit to see Leeds and London traffic sent south from Edinburgh wholly *viâ* Carlisle instead of half *viâ* Berwick. But this would naturally be the interest of the amalgamated Company.

Now if all this is obvious to an outside observer, it must be tenfold more evident to the directors and officials of the East Coast lines. In some form or another, therefore, they are certain to oppose. But their opposition may take either of two forms. They may resist the amalgamation outright. If they do, they will in all probability defeat it; for it is not easy to see how an over-strong case, regarding the matter from the point of view of the public interest, can be made in its favour. The South-Western is no bankrupt local line, unable to stand alone; it is a concern of a respectable size, which for half a century back has served and served well the whole south-west district of Scotland, and paid a reasonable dividend to its proprietors all the time. It is not a natural extension or complement of the North British; on the contrary, it occupies an entirely distinct portion of the country. Any one can see that the two companies may gain by the amalgamation; but where the profit to the public comes in is not equally clear. On the other hand, the East Coast companies may say: "The interests of the public are not our business; it belongs to Parliament to defend them. It is our business to look after the interests of our own traffic." And, acting on this principle, they may content themselves with securing over the whole of the amalgamated system powers such as it has been said they already possess over certain portions of the Caledonian. If this were insisted on, it is conceivable that the North British might prefer to withdraw their Bill altogether.

But we are not yet at the end of the obstacles with which the amalgamation scheme is confronted. The Caledonian has put forth a manifesto in which it declares that it sees no reason why the South-Western should cease to exist as an independent company. But if, it continues, this change is, in the interest of the South-Western shareholders, to take place, then it claims that the undertaking shall be transferred, not to the North British alone, but to the North British and the Caledonian jointly. In effect it says this: "Parliament has sanctioned the existence of three companies, B, the Caledonian in the middle, and A and C, the North British and South-Western, competing with it on either side. Now A and C propose to combine to crush B. We appeal to Parliament that such a combination would not only be injurious to the public interest, but unjust to us."

The claim is undeniably a strong one, and there are of course abundant precedents for the alternative course which the Caledonian proposes. Several instances have been given a few pages back of two competing companies owning lines in common. To these might be added, in Scotland, the Dundee and Arbroath, and the Kilsyth and Bonnybridge, which are joint Caledonian and North British property. In England there are the Cheshire lines; the joint Great Northern and Great-Eastern line from March to Doncaster; the joint Great-Northern and North-

Western line from Market Harborough to Newark; the Birkenhead and Shrewsbury and Hereford lines, which belong jointly to the Great Western and the North-Western; and many more. But the Caledonian claim appeals not only to the justice of Parliament. It appeals also to the self-interest of the South-Western shareholders. The North British offers to guarantee to them 4 per cent. in perpetuity. The security is doubtless ample, but a security cannot be too good, and the additional guarantee of the Caledonian would make it even more unimpeachable. Whatever other interests they may have, as South-Western ordinary shareholders at least, they stand to win something without the possibility of losing anything, if they can transfer their undertaking, not to the North British only, but to the two companies jointly. Whether, in case they vote for this, the North British will not draw back from their offer altogether, and leave them in their present position as an independent company, is of course an entirely separate question.

To sum up, I will venture on prophecy this far, that the amalgamation of the North British and the South-Western *sans phrase*, as proposed last July, is not likely to receive the sanction of Parliament. But whatever be the upshot of the affair, it has already had important indirect consequences. It has stirred up the Caledonian to a fiercely aggressive policy in return. Last session that company obtained powers for an underground line through Glasgow from east to west. This year it has a Bill to form a whole network of connecting lines and junctions at either end of it. Not only this, but a subsidiary company is seeking permission to duplicate the North British line along the right bank of the Clyde, through Dumbarton to Helensburgh, with a branch up the Vale of Leven to Loch Lomond. There will be a rival fleet of steamers on the lake, and what is more important, sidings into all the great works where is manufactured and dyed almost all the "Turkey red" that is used in the habitable world. Then again the Caledonian is applying for power to carry its Edinburgh line forward in tunnel right under the heart of the city to Leith, and so rob the North British of the cream of the traffic of that rapidly rising seaport. The long-looked-for application for powers to build a new line parallel to the South-Western along the Ayrshire coast has not come this winter, but is hardly likely to be postponed much longer.

But enough of this. Let us now see something of the special features of the existing arrangements, more especially of the competition for the summer traffic to the innumerable watering-places along the Firth of Clyde, which has given rise to what is probably the most creditable combination of railway and steamboat services in the world.

III. SOME MODERN SPECIALITIES.

THERE is a remarkable similarity between the natural situation of Glasgow and that of London. In each case, a hill, thrown out as a spur from the higher ground behind it, and rising up amidst wide marshes and lagoons surrounding its base, afforded a natural site for a cathedral and the town which grew up under its shadow. In each case a road leads down from the hill to what has for centuries been a bridge, but was once a ford, marking what, in the case of London at least, was the lowest point at which the river could in early times be crossed, thus constituting the town the natural emporium of the trade of the district. As in London the Strand, so in Glasgow Argyle Street marks the distance to which the river, even in quite modern times, extended inland. In each case, the marshes have left behind them a legacy of fog, which in Glasgow is aggravated, even more than in London, by the smoke of innumerable factory chimneys. Excepting, however, the fog, everything in Glasgow is on a smaller scale. In size and volume of water the Clyde can no more vie with the Thames than

St. Mungo's can compare with St. Paul's. But Glasgow has one enormous advantage in return. If the Clyde is narrower, it is also shorter; and within five-and-twenty miles of Glasgow there is a sea coast, which for beauty and variety can almost claim comparison with Norway itself.

From the very early days of steam travelling, the Clyde has been always in the van of progress. As long ago as 1812, more than two years before ever a steamer had been seen on the Thames, the *Comet*, of 25 tons and 3 horse-power, was plying regularly thrice a week between Glasgow, Greenock, and Helensburgh, up one day and down the next. There is nowadays a whole fleet of vessels, including amongst them the famous *Columba* and *Iona*, which daily perform the same journey at the present time; fine large saloon steamers, most of which make nothing of 20 miles an hour; but for years past the bulk of the traffic has gone by rail as far down as Greenock, and only joined the steamers there. And for the privilege of carrying it (some five-and-twenty miles each way, at a return fare of 2*s.* 6*d.* first class and 1*s.* 6*d.* third) the three great Scottish railways have long fought their hardest.

The original Greenock line, now the property of the Caledonian, was opened in 1841. Save where it turns inland for a short distance in order to reach Paisley, it follows the course of the river throughout down to its terminus in the heart of the town of Greenock. Except such as may be connected with the sugar trade, there is not much sweetness or light about the town of Greenock; and, even for Greenock, the lanes through which the passengers had to walk from the train to the steamer were more than usually noisome. But such as they were, residents "down the water" had to put up with them for nearly a quarter of a century. At last the rival company, the Glasgow and South-Western, came to the rescue. At enormous expense they formed a new line into Greenock, descending through tunnel from the high ground behind the town on to the shore, where they built a convenient pier adjoining their station. And they had their reward, for they swept away almost the whole of the Caledonian through traffic, and in a single year they have been known to carry to and from the coast over 800,000 passengers, or say every man, woman, and child, in Glasgow, Paisley, and Greenock put together; and this in spite of the fact that the Caledonian was by no means the only competing route. For a company, now merged in the all-absorbing North British, had built a line down the north bank of the Clyde to Helensburgh, while yet another railway, terminating at Wemyss Bay, cut off the great triangle of high ground near whose apex Greenock is situated, and so formed the shortest road to Innellan, as well as to Rothesay and the other places on the Island of Bute. From Wemyss Bay, too, there were steamers to Largs and to Millport, which latter place has recently had a second string to its bow with a ferry service to the new coast railway *via* Ardrossan, while, to crown the whole, the natural route for the very large traffic to the Island of Arran is the steamer service from Ardrossan Harbour, now in connection with the South-Western only, but likely before long to be competed for by the Caledonian also.

As long ago as 1865 the Caledonian saw that they must lose their "coast" traffic, unless they took active steps to retain it; so they obtained powers to continue their line forward to Gourock Bay, some three miles below Greenock. But, like many another necessary enterprise, the scheme was knocked on the head by the great panic of 1866, and the Company were left *minus* their railway, but *plus* the burden of the ownership of Gourock Harbour, to which, of course, they had no access. In 1878 the scheme was revived. After two applications had failed, in 1884 an Act was obtained; and last summer, after burrowing in a tunnel (the longest in Scotland) right under the town of Greenock, and constructing three miles of very heavy banks and cuttings, and a pier a third of a mile in length, at a total expenditure of

£600,000, the Caledonian found its bold stroke rewarded by the recovery of the bulk of the traffic which left it more than twenty years before.

And now, after this long introduction, bearing in mind that Glasgow has roughly a seventh of the population of London, and that the Glasgow fares are certainly less than half what we are accustomed to in the south, let us see the provision which is made for the conveyance of Glasgow to the sea-side on a summer afternoon. In each case we will take the crack service. At 4 P.M. the Caledonian sends off a fast train to Gourock, which calls to pick up passengers at Paisley, Port Glasgow, and Greenock. Twelve minutes later an express, which runs through without a stop, starts in pursuit, and, reaching Gourock Pier at 4.52, distributes its passengers among three different steamers which are there in waiting. Two minutes, neither more nor less, is allowed for and occupied by the transfer—no luggage is taken—and at 4.54 all three boats are under weigh, one for Loch Long, a second for the Holy Loch, and a third straight down the Firth for Rothesay, where it is due to arrive at 5.49. In the 97 minutes passengers have travelled 26 miles by train, 14 miles by boat, and have been delayed, not only by a slack through facing points at Paisley, by collecting tickets at Fort Matilda, and by the transfer at Gourock, but also by calling at four intermediate piers. As this is the last new service, with the newest boats* and the most convenient pier, it may no doubt be the smartest, but the others have no need to blush at a comparison.

At 4.10, the North British despatches its express from Queen Street to Craigendoran Pier, outside Helensburgh (also with a slightly slower pick-up train in front), and three minutes after its arrival two steamers set off to distribute its passengers. At 4.20, a second express follows; again a pair of boats are in attendance, so that amongst the four every watering-place can be served with the least possible delay. Meanwhile, at 4.15 and 4.35, a pair of trains have started for the Wemyss Bay line, to connect at the pier with a pair of steamers, the one for Rothesay, the other for Largs and Millport. Last, but by no means least, the South-Western has its 4.10 express for Greenock, with its two attendant steamers; its 4.7 for

---

* The Caledonian had a Bill in Parliament last session to enable them to run steamers of their own. So had the Glasgow and South-Western. The Caledonian Bill was thrown out, and the South-Western was in consequence withdrawn. The splendid new Caledonian boats do not therefore belong to the Railway Company, but to the Caledonian Steam Packet Company, Limited; in other words, a syndicate of Caledonian shareholders with a Caledonian director, Lord Breadalbane, as their chairman. Similarly there is a North British Steam Packet Company, Limited, owning the boats which run in connection with North British trains, both on the Clyde and on Loch Lomond.

Eleven Trains and Thirteen Boats. 89

Fairlie Pier and Largs, and its 4.20 for the steamer to Arran *via* Ardrossan. One other South-Western train well deserves mention. The 4.15 to Ayr, one of the heaviest expresses in Great Britain, has no steamboat connection, and no competition either by boat or rail. But for all that, spite of calling at Paisley, "slipping" at Irvine, and collecting tickets at Prestwick, it covers its $40\frac{1}{2}$ miles in the level hour. It should be added that the first-class fare is 5s.—to Brighton, 10 miles further, it is just double—and that Glasgow is chronically grumbling at the amount as extortionate.

In all, 11 trains, and 13 boats in connection, run for the accommodation of passengers leaving Glasgow in the half hour after 4 o'clock. On Saturdays the whole of this elaborate mechanism begins to work some two hours earlier. Needless to say, it has also to be set in motion every morning to get people up to business by half-past nine; while on Mondays, in particular, the crush is so tremendous that a special relief service has to be organized in front of the ordinary daily service. Even so, the train booked to leave Gourock at 8.30 has sometimes had to be despatched in four portions. To show the fierceness and the closeness of the competition, it is perhaps worth while giving some of the results in the form of a table.

GLASGOW AND "THE COAST."

COMPARISON of the TIMES taken by the MORNING and AFTERNOON EXPRESS TRAINS of the undermentioned COMPANIES in the SUMMER of 1889.

	CALEDONIAN *via* Gourock.		GLASGOW AND S. WESTERN *via* Greenock.		NORTH BRITISH *via* Craigendoran.		CALEDONIAN *via* Wemyss Bay.	
	Minutes.		Minutes.		Minutes.		Minutes.	
	Up	Down	Up	Down	Up	Down	Up	Down
Kilcreggan	55	47	70	60	57	55		
Cove	63	55	80	70	69	65		
Blairmore	70	62	85	75	84	75		
Strone	67	61	95	85	77	73		
Kilmun	80	73	105	100	..	..		
Ardenadam	75	67	100	90	84	80		
Hunter's Quay	60	55	..	..	72	68		
Kirn	63	55	75	60	69	65		
Dunoon	70	62	80	65	74	70		
Innellan	85	77	85	70	94	90	70	65
Rothesay	105	97	105	95	114	110	80	80
Train Time	40	40	45	40	37	37	50	50
Railway Distance	26¼ miles		25½ miles		22½ miles		30¼ miles	

It should be added that though the Wemyss Bay line looks on paper far and away the best to Rothesay, it has been seriously handicapped by the use of a much less convenient station in Glasgow. However, last autumn it was bought by the Caledonian, which hitherto has only worked it—another response to the North British challenge—and it is understood that next summer will not only see its service much improved, but also its trains admitted in Glasgow into the "Central," a station which is—what central stations by no means always are—honestly entitled to its name.

But it must not be supposed that the railways exert themselves to the utmost every morning and evening only to go to sleep for the rest of the day. On the contrary, the quantity of the services is not one whit less remarkable than their quality. There called every day last August, according to a local paper which lies before me, 54 passenger steamers at the not over-famous watering-place of Kirn, and a whole bevy of extra boats on Saturdays and Mondays. Most of them only run to and from the different railway piers, but the number is swelled by the boats which, from the stately *Columba*, or *Lord of the Isles*, down to the humble cheap tripper —sixty miles out and home for sixpence—constantly touch in the course of their complicated voyage from and to Glasgow.

There is one very remarkable feature about this "coast" traffic. The great bulk of the passengers are not season-ticket holders, but take an ordinary return ticket every time they travel. Not but what the Scottish companies are liberal enough in the conditions on which they issue their "seasons." The usual English rule is to grant them only for a minimum period of three months and—in the south of England at least—only to first and second-class passengers. In Scotland not only are third-class "seasons" universal, but they can be obtained for any length of time, from a week or a fortnight upwards, that is desired. If, after taking a ticket for a month, the owner wishes to prolong his stay at the seaside for another fortnight or three weeks, he can always extend the currency of his ticket on paying a proportional amount in excess. But, spite of this liberal treatment, the "coast" passengers prefer to take tickets every day. The reason is obvious. The ordinary fare has been brought down so low that a "season" does not pay, unless its holder goes up and down something like six days a week. Take, for example, Wemyss Bay, as it has already been mentioned. For the 60 miles to Glasgow and back, the first-class fare is 3s. 6d.—a fare which a correspondent of the *Glasgow Herald* protested against a month or two back as exorbitant. A season-ticket costs £25 per annum, so that to make it profitable one would have to travel more than thrice a week all the year round. To Brighton, on the other hand, it is only £30, but a single journey up and down costs 15s. In other words, a man who is away from Brighton three months in the year, and only comes up to town once a week during the remaining nine, will not actually lose by taking a "season."

Of course the difference, though at first sight it appears to be a difference in the scale of charge for season-tickets, is really in the fares for ordinary traffic. The ordinary fares to the "coast" have been reduced, so to speak, to the wholesale rate already. It is not that the Brighton Company treats season-ticket holders better, but that its ordinary passengers are treated much worse. On the face of it there is no reason why, if two competing companies can earn a good livelihood by carrying first-class passengers between Glasgow and Greenock at $\frac{3}{4}d.$ a mile, and third-class passengers for half the money, a company which monopolises the whole traffic between London and Brighton should be unable to carry passengers by any of the best trains for less than $2\frac{1}{4}d.$ I am not wishing here to reproach the Brighton Company. Like other commercial undertakings, it charges what it can get. But I do really believe that railway managers will have, ere long, to face the question, whether fares between two great centres of population with a constant interchange of traffic, ought to be fixed simply on a mileage basis. No one would dream of expecting a consignment of 50 tons of grey shirting, sent down from London to Southampton for shipment, to pay at the same rate as a few pieces sent to Woking or Basingstoke for the use of the local draper. And there is no reason why the rule that applies to goods should not apply to passengers. If the Londoners who want to go to Brighton can, as they do, offer themselves for conveyance "in full train-loads," the company can evidently afford to carry them at a reduced figure. I have no expectation, I admit, of seeing introduced a third-class fare to Brighton of 2s. 6d. by all trains, though I fully believe that in a comparatively short time the initial loss would be more than compensated; but one wonders whether an experiment of a similar reduction, say, between Liverpool and Manchester, is beyond the bounds of possibility.

Hitherto it has always been the outside competition of steamers, or for short distance traffic of omnibuses or tram-cars, which has brought down railway fares seriously below the normal one penny per mile. Of course there have been short spurts of rivalry, and passengers have been carried before now between Glasgow and Edinburgh for sixpence, and from York and Manchester to London and back for half-a-crown. And what is more, in this latter case—which occurred at the time of the Exhibition of 1862—so says one who has the best right to speak with authority, "as long as summer lasted and the trains were full, we didn't lose by the transaction." But fares such as this were never meant to last. What one would like to see is a serious experiment jointly undertaken by the North-Western, the Lancashire and Yorkshire, and the Cheshire lines between Liverpool and Manchester. The fares at present are by no means particularly cheap. They are 5s. 6d., 4s., and 2s. 6d. single, and 8s., 6s., and 4s. 6d. return, for the three classes respectively; on the Greenock scale they would be a good deal less than half. Say that they were brought down to one half, how long would it be before the number of passengers carried would treble itself? Less than this increase would certainly not pay the companies. No doubt they could carry many more passengers than they do at present, simply by running longer trains and more powerful engines, and therefore at practically no additional expense. But still there would be some, so that they would positively lose by carrying double the number of passengers at half the fares, except indeed for what they might gain by stimulating the traffic through Manchester to and from places beyond.

Unquestionably the whole subject is beset with difficulties, not the least of which is that any very startling modification of this kind might tend to rouse a number of sleeping dogs which the railways may think it more prudent to let lie in peace. Still one cannot but wish to see it tackled. Vast as have been the strides with which railway improvement has advanced of recent years, in the all-important item of fares the progress has certainly not been what was anticipated by the founders of our railway system. When the Liverpool and Manchester line was opened "the fare in the better class of carriages, such as the 'Queen Adelaide' and the 'Wellington,' was five shillings, for which sum the travellers and their baggage are conveyed in omnibuses to and fro between the Company's offices in the heart of either town and the commencement of the railway, a mile or a mile and a half distant, free from any additional charge or gratuity." Nowadays, as we have seen, the first-class fare, with no allowance towards the costs of one's hansom, is sixpence more; then, as now, the second-class fare was 4*s*. It ought in fairness to be added that there was in the old days no third-class at all.

Still even so the figures are not much to boast of, especially as other countries have gone a good deal ahead of us in this particular. No country probably gives as good value for a penny a mile as do our English railways; but then, in almost every country in Europe, it is possible, either by a fourth-class as in Germany, or by the zone system, as now in Hungary, or by taking a train even slower than the *soi-disant* express, as in Belgium and elsewhere, to travel for considerably less than the level penny. There must be a vast substratum of traffic waiting to be tapped by the management which has the audacity to reduce fares (not by certain specified trains in summer, but in normal everyday working) to the level which prevails on the Greenock line. It is useless to say that it could never pay. After the experience of a generation, the Caledonian and the South-Western ought to know. The Caledonian has just spent £600,000 in order to get a better share of this low-fare traffic, spite of the fact that it only lasts for four months, and the cream of it only for two; while the South-Western is likely, so common report says, to carry its line forward past Gourock to the Cloch in order once more to over-trump its rival.

Before we leave the "coast," where we have too long lingered, we must notice that the traffic is by no means merely residential. Probably nowhere in the world, certainly nowhere in the United Kingdom, are so many pleasure-tours organized with so much intelligence and forethought. Coaches and steamers are independent of the railways, but it is always possible to obtain through tickets at the railway booking-offices, and with the accounting that goes on afterwards through the companies' audit office the passenger need in no way concern himself. Take this as a fair sample of a complicated tour. Leave Glasgow about 8.30 A.M. by any of the three lines—there are expresses in connection about an hour earlier from Edinburgh—catch the *Lord of the Isles* an hour later at or near Greenock, and travel with her through the Kyles of Bute and as far as Inverary. Thence back across Loch Fyne in a small ferry steamer to St. Catherine's, whence an attendant coach will take you in a couple of hours through Hell's Glen to the head of Loch Goil, in time to catch a third steamer for Gourock, Greenock, or Craigendoran—according to the railway you have elected to patronize—and so to Glasgow in ample time for dinner. Fare for the whole round only 11 shillings. Or if this does not offer sufficient variety, you may leave the *Lord of the Isles* at Dunoon, take the coach to Inverchapel at the foot of Loch Eck, steam up the Loch, and then, with a second coach to Strachur, intercept the big vessel again on her way to Inverary. And any of these tours, of which the above is only one sample out of a hundred, may be made either way, or picked up at any point on the round. As for Loch Lomond, there is no reason why four friends, living at Carlisle, Oban, Berwick, and Dundee respectively, all agreeing to make the tour the same day, should not meet, either on board the steamer on the Loch, or at lunch at the Trossachs Hotel, and get back home in time for bed. The *rendezvous* would not cost them much over a five-pound note among the four.

Again it is impossible to resist drawing a comparison. There are half-a-dozen coaches which leave London every morning. They are all admirably horsed and turned out, and nearly always empty. Nor are the reasons far to seek. A drive for the best part of an hour through London streets and London suburbs is not attractive for one thing; for another the coaches are little known, and evidently cannot afford to advertise extensively for themselves. Is it impossible for our London railways to organize coach tours in connection with their own lines? There is no difficulty in suggesting possible routes. Guildford to Dorking along the Merrow Downs would be one; Windsor to Virginia Water through the Great Park might obviously be another. The Metropolitan might do worse than introduce its new line to public notice by opening up the beauties of the Chilterns with a coach from Chesham to Aylesbury; and even the Chatham and Dover might induce a few people to use its Maidstone and Ashford line if it brought them back by road through the beautiful country which lies between Ashford and Sevenoaks. We cannot bring the Firth of Clyde to London, but even in the way of steamboat excursions it is possible that a trip, for instance, to Dover, thence by sea to Margate or Sheerness, and so back, or again by train to Southend, steamer thence, and rail back from Margate, might attract some people on whom the delights of Ramsgate sands have begun to pall. I have no wish to teach railway managers their business, but when one sees how much the Scottish railways, which after all are principally goods lines, do to encourage pleasure traffic, and how little is done by our southern lines, which really have nothing else to distract their attention, one cannot but think that it is at least worth while calling attention to the subject.

One point more before we leave the Clyde.

Greenock does not deal only in "coast" traffic; it is one of the chief centres in the world of the sugar-refining industry. It got a hold of this trade a century or so back, when West Indian sugar was brought in to fill the gap caused by the loss of the tobacco trade with the revolted American colonies; and it has held on to it since, though nowadays the raw sugar comes mainly from the Continent, and is imported either through Leith or Grangemouth. Most people know that there was an extraordinary rise in the price of sugar a year ago. Within a few weeks raw sugar advanced from thirteen to twenty-three shillings per cwt. Last spring there were literally miles of trucks loaded with some 6000 tons of raw sugar standing in every siding in the neighbourhood of Greenock waiting for the refiners to take delivery. In response to my enquiry as to the reason of this block, I learnt that, though the raw material had advanced so largely, there had been no corresponding rise in the price of refined sugar, and that therefore, thinking the rise must come, the refiners had postponed sales till their warehouses were chock-a-block, and they were forced to use the railway company's trucks as supplementary store-rooms. There was at least one advantage in so doing, that they paid no rent.

Not so many years back the railway rate for sugar from Grangemouth to Greenock was 6s. 8d.

per ton; from Leith it was 7s. As the sugar trade became more and more depressed, the Company made reduction after reduction in the rate, till finally they had brought it down to 3s. 6d. and 3s. 9d. But when sugar almost doubled in value last spring, they thought that they too had a right to a little better terms, so they advanced the rate by 3d. per ton all round. Whether this was one of the instances of extortionate increase of which some of the Traders' Associations have made so much recently, I know not; but this I do know, and as the instance is probably unique, it is worth recording. When the agitation against the new classification and schedule of *maximum* rates first began last spring, a deputation of the Greenock sugar-refiners waited upon the general manager of the Caledonian, not in order to demand any concession, but to express their gratitude for the treatment they had received in the past, their readiness to support the Company to the utmost of their power, and their confidence that their relations with it would be equally amicable in the future. Indeed, whatever be the reason, whether that the near neighbourhood of that great anti-monopolist, the sea, has protected the traders, or whether they have defended themselves by their own superior determination and intelligence, or possibly that the Scottish railways are naturally more virtuous than their neighbours to the south, there is much less general discontent with railway rates in Scotland than in England. Alone of all the great towns of the kingdom, the Glasgow Chamber of Commerce has not appeared as an objector before the Board of Trade at the Railway Rates Enquiry.

It is not a little remarkable that the Companies who organize, and the public who enjoy, a service as admirable as that down the Clyde, are content to put up with the half-hearted service which exists between Glasgow and Edinburgh. It is not for want of competition that it is so poor. The North British has two routes, the old original Edinburgh and Glasgow line *viâ* Falkirk, and a new low-level one through Bathgate; while the Caledonian has a third through Holytown and West Calder. The distances are $47\frac{1}{4}$, $44\frac{1}{4}$, and 46 miles respectively. The Caledonian service, which has one train in 64 minutes, and a good many more only taking 65, is in point of speed distinctly the best of the three. Even the Caledonian, however, labels "express," and, what is more, charges extra for, a train which takes 85 minutes on its journey, and makes eight intermediate stops every day of the week, and a ninth on Wednesdays. On the North British I was privileged a short time back to pay express fare by a through train *viâ* Bathgate, which was allowed 2 hours and 2 minutes for $46\frac{1}{4}$ miles, and took it all with something over. On the old road the best train is timed to take 70 minutes, and quite a number of the "expresses" take 85.* In fairness, an allowance of 5 minutes must be made off this for the incline through the Cowlairs Tunnel, which, though only a mile and a half in length, descends into Queen Street Station in Glasgow with such a precipitous gradient, that it has to be worked to the present day with a stationary engine and a wire rope, so that 8 minutes instead of 3 are required for its passage. Still, once clear of Cowlairs, there is, before the train need stop again at the Haymarket Station, a run of 44 miles as straight as an arrow, and so level that in the old days it used to be said that it was difficult to keep the ballast properly drained. If a train really wants 70 minutes over this bit of road, at least it should be honestly described an "ordinary passenger," and not allowed to profane the name of "express."

Talking of Queen Street Station, it is worth notice, as showing the marvellous strides which Glasgow has made in half a century, that the

* The ingenuous confidence of Parliament is at times not a little amusing. The Edinburgh and Glasgow fares are up to their legal maximum. Parliament authorized the extra 1s. for "express," but forgot to define what express was. Similarly, in fixing 4d. per mile as the maximum first-class fare on certain lines in the south of England, it neglected to insert a further provision forbidding the application of a large I to the doors of discarded third-class vehicles.

ground on which it stands—one of the best sites in the town—was bought by the Edinburgh and Glasgow Railway in 1838 for a guinea per square yard, or to be exact, 33,128 yards (nearly seven acres) for £35,379 15s. 5d. The Company, however, only paid down the odd money, and it was not till 1846 that they were able to raise and pay off the balance of £30,000. What those seven acres are worth to-day may be judged from another sale which has recently taken place within a few yards. The Corporation of Glasgow disposed of a single acre of land in 1787 to a certain Robert Smith for £645 1s. 4d. Robert Smith at the time of the sale had a daughter six weeks old. Within her lifetime—she lived to be 98—the Corporation bought it back again as the site of their new Municipal Buildings, and the price they paid amounted to £172,944 8s. 5d. No wonder that railway debentures are generally looked upon as sound investments.

The other two Glasgow lines would have been fortunate if they had secured an access to the heart of the City at so reasonable a rate. Both the Caledonian and the Glasgow and South-Western have got nowadays fine large stations, at least as convenient and accessible as Queen Street, but the cost to their shareholders is to be reckoned not in thousands, but in millions. No doubt the game has been worth the candle. When St.

Enoch's, the South-Western Station—the ditto of St. Pancras on a somewhat smaller scale—was opened fifteen years ago, the average number of trains in and out in the 24 hours was 111. Last summer, on busy days, it reached 350. The Central station of the Caledonian is even more modern, but already not only the station but its approaches have had to be enlarged, as the trains have increased from under one hundred to over four.

The Caledonian have, however, at Buchanan Street, a second terminus, now used only for the trains to the north, and certain suburban services. Here there is a low wooden shed, put up by Joseph Locke as long ago as 1849 as a temporary structure, but still standing, and to confess the truth, except for its looks, by no means a bad station even now. How the Caledonian got there is a curious story. Their original terminus was, as has been said, at St. Rollox on the high ground to the north-east of Glasgow (where, by the bye, an old resident informs me he remembers "seeing the engines going about with mortgagees' names upon them after the crash of 1848"). Amongst other inconveniences, outside the station was a toll-gate through which passengers had to pass on their way to and from the centre of the town, so the Company determined that they must come further in. A local engineer projected a scheme by which the line was to be brought in on a viaduct with a falling gradient of 1 in 40 or thereabouts, and even then terminating at a height far above the roofs of the adjacent houses. Some of the arches were actually constructed, when the directors took alarm at what might happen if a train ran away through the station. So the building was stopped, and Joseph Locke called in. He at once decided that it was necessary to go back a mile or so behind St. Rollox, and then tunnel through the hill, and so come down more gradually to the level in Buchanan Street. But the job was a ticklish one. The new line had to be carried under the Monkland Canal and over the Cowlairs Tunnel of the Edinburgh and Glasgow Railway, and there was only very scant room for it to pass between them. The task was safely accomplished, but the engineers had an anxious time of it when the water of the canal actually began to trickle down into their workings.

Edinburgh often boasts its superiority to Glasgow. In one respect at least—its railway stations—it must acknowledge its vast and apparently hopeless inferiority. The Caledonian Station is a wooden shanty. As for the North British, in its original prospectus, dated August, 1843, it expressed its determination "to avoid all useless expense in ornamental works at stations or otherwise," and its worst enemy will scarcely deny that it has kept its promise. The Haymarket Station, the original terminus of the Edinburgh and Glasgow which was opened in 1842, has remained untouched, except the platforms—it may have been painted, but it shows no signs of it—for almost half a century. As for Waverley, what pen could do justice to it? Mr. Foxwell has tried in his recent book,* but he acknowledges the inadequacy of his own description. Not that it is, I think, quite fair to throw the whole blame upon the Company. For Haymarket they must take the responsibility, but to render the Waverley Station adequate for its traffic is beyond their powers.

It is cooped in on all sides by walls of rock. The natural way to extend it would imply an entrenchment upon a portion of Princes Street Gardens, and this the Corporation refuses to permit on any terms.† It is really rather an interesting point, in what Mr. Ruskin would call "the relation of art to use." Unquestionably the gardens are beautiful, and a railway station unlovely; but after all, the Princes Street hotelkeepers and shopkeepers would hardly wish to be left in solitude to enjoy the

---

* 'Express Trains, English and Foreign,' p. 60.

† It is suggested to me that the Company might banish the goods traffic entirely from Waverley and its immediate neighbourhood. Not having been there since the suggestion was made, I cannot say anything for or against; but unquestionably if the North British can by any possibility improve the place they will be wise to do so, and that speedily, for an additional ten minutes of Waverley will take all the taste of the Forth Bridge out of the mouth of the most enthusiastic traveller.

spectacle. Next year, when the Forth Bridge is open, the Company will scarcely venture to expose its passengers to the accustomed blocks in getting through Edinburgh. How would Edinburgh, with its metropolitan dignity, like it, if next summer some of the London expresses halted for half a moment outside the town at Millerhill Junction, contemptuously uncoupled a carriage or two, and then ran on by the suburban line direct to the Forth Bridge?

There is nothing special to note about the local traffic of Edinburgh. It is all in the hands of the North British, and consequently there are none of those prodigies of energy which are so profusely displayed in the neighbourhood of Glasgow. Nor has the North British, except on the Glasgow line, of which we have just spoken, any great opportunity of exhibiting remarkable speed. Northwards, the neck at Larbert renders such attempts impossible. Eastwards to Berwick, the expresses are "horsed," in pursuance of an old agreement, by the North-Eastern. There remains only the Waverley route southwards to Carlisle through Melrose and Hawick, and this is so bad a road that any very high speed is out of the question.*
I travelled over it not long since on the engine of

* A driver, however, told me not long since that he had taken a saloon behind his engine from Edinburgh to Carlisle, 98¾ miles in 105 minutes.

the 10.45 A.M. up express. Hardly were we clear of the complexities of the suburban branches, when we had to stop at Hardengreen for the "bank" engine to come on behind and push us up the long climb, nearly 10 miles of 1 in 70 to the top of the Fala moors, over 800 feet above sea-level. The summit reached, the bank-engine fireman comes forward along the frame of his engine and uncouples, and without a check we continue our course, gathering speed as, for fifteen miles down the Gala Water, we thread the endless loops of the stream, till the tall chimneys of Galashiels come in sight, and with a whirr the brakes go down and we pull up at the platform, 33½ miles in 49 minutes. Two minutes for a drink of water, sorely needed after her long climb, and we are off once more, and, with just a passing glimpse of Abbotsford, are over the Tweed and into Melrose. Another fifteen miles of what on the Waverley route passes for level road brings us to Hawick and the banks of the Teviot. Then again a second engine comes to our aid, for we have to cover another ten miles worse than before, up the valley of the Slitrig, with not only the gradient against us, but with curves so sharp that the driving-wheels grind against the check-rails, now on one side and now on the other. However, at length we are through the Shankend Tunnel, over a thousand feet above sea-level, and emerge into daylight on the slopes of

Liddesdale. As we rush down into the wider Eskdale, we pass place after place famous in Border story. Here it is Canobie Muir; anon it is Netherby Hall; but there is no " mounting 'mong Græmes of the Netherby clan," only an old cock-pheasant lazily sunning himself in the line, whose dignity hardly suffers him to move on till the wheels are within a yard of catching him. Another moment and we are speeding across Solway Moss. Ten minutes more, " the sun shines fair on Carlisle wall," and our journey is over. The engine moves off to its "stable," to wait till it is time for the return journey, but not a solitary passenger troubles himself so much as to put his head out of the window and cast a look at the steed that has carried him so well.

For all that, the run, $98\frac{1}{4}$ miles in just over two hours and a half, or roughly 39 miles an hour with three intermediate stoppages, is not a little remarkable. On the Continent they would label it "express, first class only," if it was 10 miles an hour slower across the dead levels of Burgundy or Brabant. What the *Chemin de Fer du Nord* authorities, who cannot manage to keep time with their expresses from Paris to Amiens at some 40 miles an hour, would think of hauling over this road the heavy Pullmans of the Midland down Highland express, in 140 minutes without a stop, one really would like to know. Probably they would think what a nuisance competition was, to force officials to take all this trouble for a public which after all was as discontented as ever.

And now let us get back to Edinburgh in a very different and much more leisurely fashion. In no trade have railways made a greater revolution than in the cattle trade. Great fairs, such as that at Falkirk, held at long intervals, are dying out, and their place is being taken by regular weekly markets in the chief railway centres, such as Edinburgh or Perth. The market-day in Edinburgh is Tuesday, so one Monday night I slept in Berwick in order to come up with a cattle train the following morning. We—the engine and the brake, for there were no cattle—set off from Berwick at 6.45, and climbed up on to the cliffs as the sun was coming out over the North Sea. But in spite of the sun the brakesman and his passenger were not sorry when the fire in the stove began to burn up. At four stations, one after the other, the signal was "off," as a sign that there was nothing for us that morning, so on we ran. After an hour had thus been spent to no purpose, I was forcibly reminded of the story of Napoleon's cutlet. Napoleon's taste was of the simplest; he never wanted anything but a cutlet, but he always expected a cutlet to be ready for him at whatever moment he might happen to want it. The arrangement might be convenient, but was scarcely economical, as not a few cutlets were wasted. And so if our British farmers expect to have a special train run past their doors on market-day, on the chance that they may have a beast or two ready for the butcher, they can hardly expect to get their service as cheap as if they had to give a couple of days' notice of their intention.

At length at Cockburnspath, 21 miles from Berwick, we picked up a couple of trucks, at Innerwick three more, and at Dunbar again three. Then, after drawing two stations blank, at Drem, the junction for North Berwick, we made a great haul, and completed our load with three and twenty trucks all at once; so we had only to wait till the up passenger train had passed us, and then make the best of our way to market; a second special must pick up the stock from the remaining stations. Travelling in a goods brake has, it must be honestly admitted, not many advantages over a first-class carriage, but it has one conspicuous merit. On a passenger train one may be late—indeed, if one is privileged to live on the Chatham and Dover, one not unfrequently is—but one cannot possibly be early. A goods train goes ahead, as soon as it has done its work and the line is clear. On this occasion, thanks to the Drem farmers and their twenty-three trucks, we reached our destination more than half an hour before we were due.

As we approached Niddrie, the junction with the Waverley line, we saw another cattle train coming up from Hawick which ought by rights to have preceded us. But it was too late; we had "got the road," and could not be dislodged from our pride of place. Behind the Hawick train was another, which had started at 5 o'clock from Carlisle, and picked up the traffic from the further side of Hawick. Later on, when we got nearer Haymarket, where the sales are held, we encountered other trains from Fife, and from Greenhill and the north. In all, 130 to 150 truck-loads is no uncommon consignment for a Tuesday morning. Arrived at the cattle dock, the animals were walked out of their trucks almost as easily and quickly as a train-load of passengers, and off into the covered yards of the different salesmen. Hardly are they out of the trucks, when men with great jets of water from a fire-hose set to work to wash out the trucks, and to cover the floor with layers of fresh sawdust, brought up in truck-loads from the carriage shops at Cowlairs; and then everything is ready for the animals to commence their journey, about 5 o'clock in the afternoon, to whatever great town of England their purchasers may consign them.

There is another though less necessary article of food than meat, which the North British deals with in wholesale quantities, and that is mushrooms. It comes about in this wise. The old Edinburgh,

I

Perth, and Dundee line, coming up from the Granton and Burntisland ferry, got into Waverley Station by a tunnel under St. Andrew's Square and Princes Street. It was about three-quarters of a mile long, and the gradient was so steep as to necessitate the employment of a stationary engine. Of late years a *détour* out to the east has avoided the gradient, and the tunnel has been abandoned. For a long while it was simply useless, or rather worse than useless to the Company, for it was alleged that disabled trucks, from the Scotland Street end, where the old station is now used as a coal depôt, used to be shunted into the tunnel out of the way, and so lost to sight and forgotten. Two years back an ingenious person conceived the idea of leasing the tunnel and growing mushrooms. The company were not too exacting about terms. Any rent was better than no rent, and moreover they got the carriage of all the materials for forming hot-beds inwards, and all the mushrooms that were grown out again. And what with soil and manure, the grower declares that he uses up a train-load of stuff in a twelvemonth. Even the very spawn comes in, a truck-load at a time.

When I was there, one bitter cold day last March, I found a huge fire of anthracite burning just inside the lower mouth of the tunnel, which was only closed by a wooden screen, movable so as to permit the passage of railway trucks. In this way

The Mushroom Company, Limited. 115

the chill was taken off the air as it entered. The upper, or Waverley Station, end of the tunnel is built up with brickwork. Throughout the entire length there runs a double line of rails. What used to be the up line is kept clear for use, as the beds have to be removed bodily and renewed about every six months. But between this line and the wall there is a small border carried along throughout, and the place of the down line is occupied by a series of beds running across at right angles. For a hundred yards one walks along a set of beds in full bearing. Then again a second set have just been made, but are still too hot and rank for the spawn to be put into them. A little further one comes upon a gang of men, at work by the light of lanterns in making up a third set. I learnt that, at the time of my visit, the French growers had not yet got their produce into the market, and that the Edinburgh Mushroom Company, Limited, could obtain from the salesmen from 1$s.$ to 1$s.$ 9$d.$ a pound, and even at that price had more orders than they were able to execute.

With this, which is, I cannot but think, one of the strangest developments of railway working, let us leave the beaten highways of Lanarkshire and Midlothian, in order to make a circuit through the less familiar regions of Aberdeenshire and the Highlands.

IV. The Great North and the Highland.

The Great North of Scotland and the Highland are two railways that at first sight seem to have much in common. In length of line they are not very unlike, as the Highland has 425 and the Great North 316 miles; while in train mileage they are practically identical, as each company runs between 850,000 and 900,000 miles in the half year. The capital too in each case is about four and a half millions sterling. Further, in each case the staple of the traffic consists of sheep, cattle, and fish, reinforced in the summer by an enormous influx of passenger traffic, both sportsmen and tourists. Spite, however, of this superficial resemblance, the position of the two companies is very dissimilar. The Highland is all main line, the Great North all branches, a difference which of course rests upon a difference in the territory which they respectively occupy. In all the 300 miles from Perth to Wick, except perhaps for the stretch from Forres to Dingwall, there is hardly a square mile of really fertile ground: Aberdeen and Banff, on the other hand, are perhaps at the present time the most prosperous agricultural districts in Great Britain. Yet again, in the Highland territory there is hardly such a thing as a manufactory; the very hides of the beasts killed for the London or Glasgow markets go south to be tanned: Aberdeen has a number of flourishing industries.

The nearest analogue to the Great North is possibly to be found in the Great Eastern. Substitute Aberdeen for London, and reduce the scale throughout somewhat in similar proportion, writing Keith and Elgin for Cambridge and Norwich, Peterhead and Fraserburgh for Yarmouth and Lowestoft, Banff and Lossiemouth for Cromer and Felixtowe, and the Braemar Highlands for the Norfolk Broads, and you have no bad idea of the Great North position. There is another respect in which the analogy applies. The Great North, like the Great Eastern, has turned over a new leaf of recent years, and resolutely set itself to live down the reputation acquired by long and patient continuance in ill-doing. That the reputation was well deserved in the case of the Great North, there can be no question. Many are the stories told of its despotic treatment of passengers, who after all were neither foes nor criminals. For one thing, its management steadily refused to effect a junction with the line to Perth and the south. Though invited to take a share in the construction of the present joint station, and to extend their line into it, they persisted in remaining at Waterloo Station, which is now their goods depôt, a long way off down the quay, and thither all passengers for the north had to transfer themselves and their luggage. Not only so, but the Great North train was timed to leave almost immediately after the south mail arrived, and passengers who failed to get across as quickly as the mail bags were sternly shut out and relentlessly left behind. On one occasion a director of the company, finding himself locked out with the rest, and refusing to accept his fate with resignation, smashed a window and got in that way.* Another time, Mr. Merry, a Scottish M.P. well known in his day, had the mortification of seeing his wife and family go on without him, a disappointment which he caused the company to regret some years after, when they found him upon a Parliamentary Committee to which a Great North Bill had been referred. Indeed the very first appearance of the Great North on the scene in 1852 was in an attitude which was hardly con-

* The *Aberdeen Free Press* has been good enough to characterize this story as undoubtedly belonging to the region of myth. It was told me, however, by a very well-known resident in Aberdeen as a fact within his own knowledge. Till therefore the *Free Press* can prove that it did not happen, I shall continue to believe it.

ciliatory. It had been permitted by Parliament to acquire possession of the Aberdeen and Inverurie Canal, then the main highway of the traffic of the district. Having got it, it promptly proceeded to let the water out, in order to obtain access to Aberdeen along the canal bed.

The Great North has, however, outgrown these youthful indiscretions. Perhaps no line, not even the Lancashire and Yorkshire, can boast of more rapid improvement in recent years. A decade back every train stopped at every station, and to get to Elgin, 80 miles from Aberdeen, took at least $4\frac{1}{4}$ hours. To-day, though the fastest trains are run by a route 7 miles longer, they cover the distance in just over $2\frac{1}{2}$ hours, or at an inclusive speed of 34 miles an hour throughout. Considering that this is mainly over single line, with five intermediate stops for certain, and five more conditional, it is really more creditable to the company than many a through train timed nearly half as fast again on an English main line. Moreover, though 34 miles an hour may not entitle a train in Great Britain to rank as express, in France it would be ample to justify the company in labelling it "rapide, première classe seulement," while in Italy or the United States they would unquestionably dignify it with the title of "Lightning Express."

Needless to say, improvements so sweeping in the

train service have not been accomplished without corresponding improvements in both engines and carriages. The new stock would do credit to any line in Great Britain, and through coaches are now sent every day in summer to Glasgow; so Lowlanders have the opportunity of judging for themselves. Indeed it is not a little remarkable how good the rolling-stock in out-of-the-way parts of the country often is. I have travelled through the length and breadth of Great Britain, from Penzance to Peterhead, from Strome Ferry to Cromer, and from Wick to Weymouth, and I can honestly say that, with a possible exception in favour of the Brecon and Merthyr, I have never, even in the most outlandish parts, come across carriages which can equal in badness those which the South-Eastern and the Chatham and Dover boldly run year after year—our grandchildren will probably, if the timbers hold together so long, be able to add, century after century—into their termini in the heart of the metropolis.

Yet more remarkable than the goodness of the Great North stock is the size of the works in which it is built. The shops at Kittybrewster —the eponymous heroine of this oddly-named place is believed to have been the keeper of an adjacent toll—were only meant to do repairs, and were much too small for that; and now that it has come to building new engines and carriages as well, it is a wonder how matters are ever kept going at all. The erecting-shop only holds four engines, and half the work has consequently to be done in the open air. Fortunately Scotchmen are contented to let pass as mist what the effeminate Southron would describe as drenching rain. The Kittybrewster engines have two specialities. In addition to the accustomed damper, they have a series of holes opening into the front of the fire-box immediately underneath the boiler, and secondly, an ingenious arrangement of the valve-gear brings the cylinders so close together that room is made for the employment of a leading bogie with wheels of exceptionally large size.

The Great North, as has been said, is all branches. There is one branch, however, that namely up Deeside, which has had one try at being a main line already, and is likely some day to repeat the attempt. A quarter of a century back, when the Caledonian was troubled with growing pains in every part of its system from Aberdeen to Greenock, it made an attempt to get hold of this line so as to continue onward its route up Deeside, thence across the hills and down one of the tributaries of the Don to Alford, and thus obtain an access to Moray and Inverness behind the back of the Great North. This latter company accordingly found itself in much the same position in which the Great Western was placed some ten years later by the attempt of the Midland to get hold of the Bristol and Exeter. It was forced in self-defence to offer still better terms, and to-day the lucky Deeside shareholders get about 10 per cent. for their money. We are not likely again to see the scheme for a line to Alford mooted, but it is an open secret, that but for the objection of an influential Aberdeenshire proprietor, who occupies Balmoral and Abergeldie Castles and a good deal of land in their vicinity, the railway would before now have been carried forward from Ballater at least as far as Braemar. Thence one bold scheme would have taken it right through the Cairngorms to Aviemore, and so on to Inverness; but that road is now in the possession of the Highland Company; so possibly an exit may be found some day down Strath Avon, where the important town of Tomantoul is clamouring for railway accommodation. Not that, to tell the truth, the traffic of Lochnagar, or Glenlivat, or the other great distilleries of the neighbourhood, is by any means a despicable item in railway receipts. Some of them are said to turn out 2000 gallons of whiskey per week. But there are cynics who declare that, yet more remarkable than the amount of whiskey sent out, is the amount imported into the district from Leith. If this be true, at least the railway need not grumble, as it must get the carriage of the traffic both ways.

Herrings, Whales, and Convicts.

The speciality of the Deeside line is its tourist traffic; the Buchan line, on the other hand, which runs due north from Aberdeen to Maud Junction, and there subdivides to serve both Peterhead and Fraserburgh, probably does not see a dozen tourists in a twelvemonth. Fraserburgh subsists mainly on herrings; Peterhead has two additional strings to its bow, whales and convicts. The convicts are occupied in constructing a harbour of refuge, a mile or so south of the town, a job that, from what I saw of the obstinacy of Peterhead granite, is likely to last them for some time to come. As for the whales, according to all precedent, they ought to come to Peterhead ships to be killed. But of late years they have shown an increasing disinclination to do so. In the last five years the value of the produce of the whale-fishing, taking Peterhead and Dundee together, has declined steadily and continuously from £88,000 in 1884 to £12,000 in 1888. Two reasons are given by the experts. The one that the ice has in recent summers never broken up sufficiently to allow the whales to be reached; the other that the animals themselves have deserted their old feeding-grounds. As we know, on the authority of Mr. Matthew Arnold, it is their custom to

> "Sail and sail with unshut eye
> Round the world for ever and aye."

One of these voyages they appear to have undertaken lately, and to have sailed through the North-West passage into the North Pacific. At least, the American fleet from San Francisco, which fishes in Behring Straits, has had very different luck from that which has befallen the Scottish fishermen off the coast of Greenland.

Perhaps as Peterhead is an out-of-the-way place, I shall not be wrong in assuming that some, at least, of my readers are as ignorant on the subject of whale-fishing as I was when I went there last spring, and so I may be pardoned if I dwell on my own experiences. I was told that Captain David Gray, one of the greatest authorities on Arctic navigation living, had caught two whales on his last voyage, and so made, at least, some profit. The whales yielded 22 tons of oil, worth about £20 per ton, say £450, and in addition, 18 cwt. of whale-bone. I expressed my surprise that so small a sum should cover expenses. "But you have not allowed," said my informant, "for the bone." "But there is only 18 cwt.; that cannot be worth much," I answered. "About £1500," was the quiet reply. I thought I must have misunderstood, but it turned out in further conversation that £1600 to £1700 a ton was the current price for whalebone, and that it had been known to fetch £2250, or say, in other words, 1s. 3d. an ounce.*

* This last autumn the American fishery has also failed and "bone" is now quoted at about £2500.

It was excusable to feel a desire to see so valuable a commodity in its natural state. I did just know that the bone (as it seems to be always called) was not bone at all, but a substance existing nowhere else in nature; that it was attached, so to speak, on a hinge, and lay inside the upper jaw of the whale; and that when he blows out the water which has been allowed to flow in through his open mouth, it falls down across it like a portcullis, and so prevents the minute creatures which form his food from escaping. But I certainly was not prepared for what I saw. The individual pieces were some of them as much as 12 or 14 feet in length. They were perhaps ten inches to a foot broad at the bottom, and tapered to a point at the top. Down the centre of each ran a strong rib, and the edges on either side were fringed with coarse hair. The weight would be some 10 lbs. or thereabouts apiece. It gave one a startling idea of the size of the animal to imagine a row of these great palisades, which would reach from the floor to the ceiling of any ordinary room, swinging up and down every minute inside his closed mouth.

Whale oil is by no means so attractive a subject of investigation as whale-bone. When the animal is killed, the blubber, or layer of fat which wraps it round and keeps it warm, is cut into great pieces, and thrown into the tanks which line the hold of the vessel throughout, and there it remains till the vessel gets home. Then it is taken out, and, under the joint influence of heat and pressure, the oil is extracted. Fresh blubber is said to be good eating, but anything more horrible than the smell of a great vat full of rancid blubber it is impossible to conceive. Whale oil, or seal oil, for they are much the same, has but one use. It all goes to Dundee to soften the jute fibres, and prevent them from breaking in the process of manufacture.

Peterhead, spite of the failure of its whale fishery, has by no means a depressed look; and this is the more remarkable, seeing that the herring industry is depressed as well. For if the town has suffered from a dearth of whales, it has suffered even more from a plethora of herrings. Five years back, in 1884, the catch was so tremendous that all the Continental markets were glutted; the price of a barrel of fish fell to a point that hardly paid for the empty cask; and only last year did the demand at length once more overtake the supply. It is strongly urged, however, by those who should know, that the loss has been caused largely by bad management. At present, the herrings, if not taken for immediate consumption, are shipped to Hamburg, there to be put into store, in order that the curers may be able to obtain advances on their bills of lading.

This, it is argued, is a radically faulty system. The interest of Hamburg is that of buyers; they will naturally wish to depress prices as low as possible. Granted that it is necessary for the curers to be able to obtain advances on their fish as soon as possible, the need should be met by the establishment in the fishing ports of a system of warrant stores, such as exists in all the great iron-producing centres. The oldest and most famous of these is Connal's store in Glasgow. Passengers into the Central Station there may notice, on their left hand just before they cross the river, a large enclosure filled with stacks of pig-iron, amounting probably, as a rule, to hundreds of thousands of tons. This is Connal's store, or at least one of them, and into it any maker may send his iron, on payment of a small sum for rent and expenses. For every 500 tons—200 tons first, and 300 tons second quality—he obtains a warrant, and on the production of this instrument, he can in a moment either sell his iron or raise money on it in any part of the world. So much do the Scottish makers appreciate the advantages of the system, and such haste do they use to avail themselves of it, that it is sometimes jocularly alleged that the railway trucks have their bottoms burnt out by the pigs that are hurried off to the store before they have had time to cool. It may be added that, if any one wishes to secure a princely income without exertion and without risk, he can hardly do better than open a warrant store. Nothing is needed except an office and a couple of clerks, and of course, in addition, a name that shall be known throughout Christendom, and a credit as unassailable as that of the Bank of England.

It is not, however, in a herring-store at home that the fishing ports of the North of Scotland have hitherto sought salvation. Rather have they tried to find it in sending away a larger portion of their catch in the form either of fresh or kippered herrings. This latter trade both at Peterhead and at Wick is at present advancing by leaps and bounds. As for wet fish, it also is going south in increasing quantities, more especially from the series of small fishing towns lying along the shore of the Moray Firth. A new railway, known as the Buckie Extension, has been opened within the last year or two, and a series of excellent small harbours has been built by the public-spirited enterprise of Lady Gordon Cathcart and other local proprietors, with the result that, from the mouth of the Spey, almost as far round as Banff, the little towns of Port Gordon, Buckie, Portessie, Portknockie, Cullen, and half a dozen more, are all as prosperous and contented as well can be. We are often told that it is the railway rates which strangle the fishing industry. It would be more accurate to say that it is to the railway rates that the fishing industry owes it that it exists at all. At Peterhead, for example, an old resident complained that, whereas he used formerly to be able to buy a fine cod for 1s., now that the fishermen could send away their catch by train, he was forced to pay not less than 2s. 6d. to 3s. 6d. As for Wick and Thurso, till the railway got there, it was never worth while catching the herrings at all, unless they were in good enough condition to be fit for curing.

Here is the evidence brought forward in favour of what is now the Highland line when it was first proposed in the year 1846. If the line were made, it is pointed out, " the haddock, cod, turbots, skates, soles, and shell-fish of the Moray Firth might be in Manchester and its neighbourhood about 12 hours after leaving the water, and the ton of fish which they now pay about £14 to £18 for, would cost them but £6 or £7, for at this moment it might be purchased at the boats for £3, and £3 more would see it unladen in Manchester market." The prophecy has turned out remarkably correct as far as the railways are concerned. Fish leaving Buckie on the Moray Firth at 1.40 by the Highland road, or twenty minutes later by the rival route, is in Manchester under 14 hours, and the rate is just about £3 a ton. But the widening of the area supplied has raised immensely the initial cost of the fish. Even herrings are worth perhaps twice £3; as for soles and turbots their value is much more like £3 per cwt. Nor does the prophet appear to have foreseen how large a sum would be needed for what the fish trade euphemistically describes as "expenses of distribution."

Let us see what the railway charges really are, and then what the companies have to do to earn them. Without going into intricate details of classification, owner's risk or companies' risk, and so forth, it will probably be sufficiently accurate to say that a ton of herrings, haddock, whiting, or cod, will be delivered in Billingsgate market from the north of Scotland—a distance of not less than 600 miles—for £4. In other words, the company receives about three halfpence for carrying a ton of fish one mile. The average rate for a ton of merchandise is probably about the same; for a ton of coal about one halfpenny. To put the figures in a form perhaps more interesting to the ordinary consumer: the cost of carriage increases the value of the 10 lb. cod, which was worth half-a-crown retail in Peterhead, to as much as 2s. 10$\frac{1}{4}d$. in London. No doubt the benevolent fishmonger deeply laments his inability to supply this fish to his hungry customers at any less price than half a sovereign; still, it is not quite fair for him to tell them that this inability is caused by the amount of the railway charges.

Of course, however, it is always possible that the rates, though only a fraction of the retail cost of the fish, do really bring in to the companies an unfair and unnecessary percentage of profit. To judge whether this is so or not, consider how the traffic is actually worked. The fishing fleet gets in, say to Peterhead and Fraserburgh, at nine o'clock in the morning. The fish are sorted out on the quay, sold by auction, packed and sent up to the station. They are loaded instantly upon trucks, and by one o'clock an engine starts from each place with perhaps 20 tons of fish. A dozen miles off at Maud Junction, the two trains of, say, 15 trucks are united, and thence they are run away straight for the markets of the south: a special train for 600 miles at express speed throughout. It will probably be a week before the empty trucks get home again. To show the solicitude with which the fish traffic is watched over, let me narrate a personal experience. I left Peterhead for London one day last spring by the 2.45 P.M. train A few miles outside Aberdeen we were stopped, and learnt that the fish special, which had started in front of us, had broken down. Matters were, however, soon put right; the fish train and the passenger train were amalgamated, and we ended in reaching Aberdeen only about 20 minutes late. Meeting there the superintendent of the line, who was on the look-out for our arrival, I expressed my regret that the London express would be delayed. "Oh, never mind the express," was his reply; "what I want to do is to get the fish special away to Perth in front of you." This in the result proved impossible, but it ran through Perth and got in front while the passenger train was marshalling. The ordinary earnings of an English goods train are about 6s. per mile. Will any one say that 5s., which would be about the gross receipts of a fish special such as that described above, is an extravagant sum?

But it is probable that the companies would be only too well satisfied to compound for an average of a good deal less. Supposing the 14 trucks had only been 8 or 9. They would still have been too much for the passenger train to take, and would have required the services of an engine to themselves. So that, in fact, while the expenditure remained constant, the receipts would have been diminished almost one-half. Yet worse, supposing the fish had never come at all. Take an actual case. The station master at a fishing port telegraphs that a heavy catch of fish is expected that morning. In hot haste an engine is ordered out, and a train of trucks got ready and sent down some 60 or 70 miles from Aberdeen. The wind changes, and the boats cannot get in, and after waiting about for hours till it is too late to think of catching the next day's market, engine and trucks go back to Aberdeen empty-handed. Here is a dead loss of say £5 to the company, which must in fairness be balanced against the £20 or £30 it will earn as its share of the receipts for the next consignment.

The Buckie Extension line from Portsoy to Fochabers is a beautiful road, but the Spey at its mouth is by no means an attractive river. To see its real beauty one must take the old inland route and cross the stream where at Craigellachie it leaves the mountains for the open plain, or better still turn up the Strathspey branch to join the Highland Railway at Boat of Garten.

Railway managers, with all their enterprise to attract tourists, hardly, I think, do as much as they might to give them the full benefit of the scenery they pass through. So at least it struck me, as I travelled one lovely day last May on the engine along the Strathspey line. Of course, the footplate of the engine—always supposing one has no special interest in the working of injectors or dampers or what not, to distract one's attention just as one ought to catch a glimpse up the mouth of a glen— is the best place possible from which to see the landscape. But then accommodation on the footplate is very strictly limited. In an ordinary railway carriage, even if one has the good luck—a thing probably not as a rule desired by railway companies—to have it all to oneself, one really sees little of the scenery through which the train passes. Even *coupés* have their outlook blocked by the end of the carriage in front. The saloons run on the Highland line are better, but the seats face inward instead of outward, and moreover, they are only available for first-class passengers. There is really no reason why "observation waggons," as the St. Gothard authorities term them, with glass sides and all the seats facing forward, should not be run on lines such as the Strathspey or the Highland, the Callander and Oban, or the Settle and Carlisle. It would of course be necessary to turn them round at the end of their journey, but there is no great difficulty in this. Further, they would have to be taken off in winter, but then there is not a line in the kingdom which has not a good deal of its rolling stock standing idle in winter even as it is.

The scenery, however, was not the only thing that impressed me that morning on Spey-side. As the train ran into Aberlour Station, there was an unusual number of people and an unusual excitement on the platform, with an amount of luggage that even in August would have been considered respectable. The large square wooden boxes with their big printed labels, "Anchor Line—not wanted on voyage," soon told their own tale. It was a party of emigrants *en route* for New York; "going away," as the engine-driver phrased it with the pathos of simplicity. Not indeed as friendless outcasts, for the laird himself — who probably knew something as to the contents of those substantial boxes — had come down to see them off, and wrung their hands as he wished them God speed; and when, a moment afterwards, the train sped unconcernedly on its way, all along the line for several miles, at the door of every cottage, from which the blue wreath of peat smoke curling up showed there was some one at home, friends had gathered to wave their hands and wish them once more good-bye. It was well, no doubt, that they should go. The "divine discontent," if one may borrow the expression, which forbids the peasant of to-day to accept the condition of his ancestors — a century ago, so a Government Inspector wrote at the time, the Aberdeenshire peasants used to save themselves from starvation by bleeding their half-starved cattle at the end of a long winter—was thrusting them out into a wider world, where fate is less stern than among the rugged Grampians. And beautiful though the valley might look, when the brilliant green of birch and larch stood out from the broom and the anemones at their feet against the dark background of firs, the scene in the long dreary months of winter, when the sun never tops the hills, and the firs claim the foreground, with no background but snow, must be quite otherwise.

One thing, however, it was impossible not to regret. The labels on the luggage were not for our own colonies, but for the United States. Where Lady Gordon Cathcart has set so good an example, other Highland proprietors at least might follow it and see that the surplus population of their straths and glens, the flower of the British army in the wars of the beginning of the century, is not lost to Greater Britain in the newer battles of commerce with which the century closes.

There was another thing which much impressed me on the Spey-side line, as it always does in every part of the Highlands, and that was the admirable postal connections. Imagine a mail leaving Aberdeen at 3.30 A.M., and picking up and putting out its bags all along the route—in order that the fishermen of the Banff coast may find their Edinburgh and Glasgow letters awaiting them when they come down to breakfast. Yet more remarkable, imagine that from Inverness to Wick, through that "desert of silence," as Mr. Foxwell appropriately terms Caithness, the Highland Company hurries the mails faster than the Italian lines can convey the international special train to Brindisi, faster than the German and the Belgian Governments, with the assistance of the *Chemin de fer du Nord*, can forward their passengers from Aix to Calais. Till some one can point out a better, I shall venture to believe that the combined rail and steamboat mail services to the Western coast, and to Skye and the Lews, are unmatched in the world.

That they do not pay directly may be taken for granted. The postal subsidy of the Great North is nearly £18,000 a year, while that of the Highland is no less than £55,000, and probably all the postage stamps used throughout their territory would not cover this sum. But for all that few would be so foolish as to grudge the money. The Postmaster-General, with his omnipresent mail bags, and his yet more obtrusive parcel-post hampers—I saw six huge ones landed from the Orkney steamer one evening last June—is a far more efficient representative of the central government than any Secretary of State for Scotland, and is doing more to cement the Union than any Scottish Home Rule League can do to break it. If one has any objection to make, it is that the Post Office does not direct towards the improvement of our intercourse with Australia and Canada the same statesmanlike liberality which it has shown in its dealings with the Highlands of Scotland.

But we must get back to Aberdeen, and without stopping to notice its cotton, linen, and jute mills, or even its more important paper works—no favourites of the lairds these, for their owners manufacture paper from Swedish wood pulp, alleging that local wood is too full of resin to be used, and then poison the trout in the streams with the refuse—we must just cast a glance at the granite quarries. Of these one of the largest and most famous is that at Kemnay, some dozen miles from Aberdeen, whence came the granite used in the construction of the great Forth Bridge.

The quarry, which is 200 feet deep, is situated on the top of a hill, and the stone, after being hoisted up from the bottom, is let down along a steep incline to the railway in trucks, which are worked by a stationary engine with a wire rope. Big blocks, and some of them are enormous, are raised with cranes, smaller ones are hoisted by an ingenious machine termed a "Blondin," but which looks not unlike a safety bicycle, that runs up and down on a wire cable stretched from top to bottom at an angle of 45°. One of these machines will run down the whole 200 feet in 18 seconds, and come back to the top, bringing with it a couple of tons of stone, in just over a minute. Sometimes, however, a successful blast detaches blocks so big that no machinery can move them, and they have to be broken up. One that we measured was 18 feet by 16 by 12, and would weigh some 300 tons. The biggest pieces mostly go into Aberdeen to be shaped into columns or tombstones or pedestals; the next size will make doorsteps or lintels; a smaller size will do for kerbstones; last of all, the fragments are broken up into "setts," as they are termed, for street pavement. As for the mere chips, which in an ordinary country would fetch a high price for road-metal, they lie about in heaps of thousands of tons, and any one who will be so good as to take them away will be warmly welcomed. I noticed that the kerbstones were being finished with what seemed to me quite unnecessary precision, for, needless to say, granite is not a material in which a workman gets very rapidly "forrarder," and asked the reason. To my surprise, the foreman replied that in this particular branch Norway was underselling Aberdeen in the London market. Unless the kerbstones were both better finished and sold for less money than used to be asked, it would be no good expecting to sell them at all. Indeed, not only London, but actually Aberdeen itself, imports foreign granite, but in this case the reason is to obtain varieties of colour that the local quarries do not afford.

We have left to the last what is after all the main industry of Aberdeenshire, namely, cattle raising. The whole district is, in the words of one of its leading agriculturalists, one great beef-factory. Not that the factory is by any means an old-established one. In 1779, Mr. Andrew Wright, who travelled through the country as surveyor to the Commissioners on the Annexed Estates, declared that it was no wonder the sheep were small, as he "could observe no grass till he alighted and put on his spectacles." In 1786 the "valued rent of the whole shyre of Aberdene" was £19,418. In these days the cattle were driven southwards to fatten. But then came the introduction of sown grasses and turnips, and in 1812 the rental of the country had risen to over £300,000. The farmers could now keep their beasts at home and fatten them themselves. But what it must have cost to get them to market—not, of course, to Manchester or London, but to Edinburgh or Glasgow—may be judged from contemporary English evidence. A beast driven up from Norfolk to London, so a tenant on the Holkham estate declared, took a fortnight on the road and lost three guineas in value. From Hockliffe in Bedfordshire, less than 50 miles from London, said a witness before a House of Lords committee in 1837, 1500 cattle and 1000 sheep are driven up weekly to Smithfield market. The charge is 7s. a head for cattle and 1s. for sheep; and, besides, the animals suffer "injury incalculable. . . . Cattle are constantly left at every town on the road, where they are sold for what they will fetch." From Braybrooke, near Market Harboro', said another witness, "the charge for driving is 7s. in summer and 8s. in winter, but he would be glad to pay 17s. for railway condition. He had always understood that a sheep driven 80 miles wasted 8 lbs., that is a stone." No wonder that the shrewd Aberdeenshire farmers were glad to avail themselves of railway transit as early as possible.

But to-day they have got far beyond the stage of merely sending the cattle of their own raising to market. The country could never raise nor even feed all the beasts which it despatches southwards. Many years back the farmers took to bringing in store cattle from Ross-shire. Then when Ross-shire learnt to fatten for itself, they went further afield and imported from Ireland. When this source of supply in turn was closed by pleuro-pneumonia, they started a company and chartered ships to fetch store cattle from Canada. And to feed the Canadian beasts and enrich the pastures over which they roam, ships from all quarters of the globe pour into the Aberdeen harbour feeding stuffs and manures. A vessel may be seen discharging bones from the River Plate alongside of another loaded with maize and cotton-cake from Baltimore, or a third freighted with locust beans from Alexandria. It shows the importance of the industry that one of the fiercest fought railway battles of this generation was the case of the Aberdeen Manure Company *v.* the Great North of Scotland, which turned on the question whether the wording of its Act of Parliament compelled the railway company to carry artificial guano, worth probably £7 or £8 a ton, at the rate which was fixed for ordinary farm-yard manure. The importance may be shown in another way. In December, 1888, the North British carried to London, for the Christmas market alone, 1016 head of cattle in six special trains composed of 96 trucks. For Christmas, 1889, the Caledonian

Company took 1048 head in 187 trucks, for the custom is that East and West Coast divide the Christmas traffic turn and turn about. In addition the Midland secured 334 head in 58 trucks. It should be added, as the cost of driving beasts in the old days has been given—7s. for 50 miles— that the modern rate per head for ten times the distance is about a sovereign.

If the Great North is pre-eminently a cattle line, the specialty of the Highland might be said to be its traffic in sheep, of which it carried last year over a quarter of a million head. But that would be only a very partial account of the matter. Railways may have done much for Aberdeenshire, but they have done far more for Ross and Cromarty and Sutherland. It is the railway, and not General Wade and his roads, that the Highlander should really lift up his hands to bless. Forty years back it cost 6s. a quarter to get the barley grown in Badenoch down to Inverness, while to bring a ton of coal up again was worth from £1 to 25s. Here is another sample from the brave days of old. "Hundreds and even thousands of packages, containing each but a few brace of birds, lie daily throughout the season waiting their turn for transmission by coach and steamer, until it would be far better that the birds had never been killed, or that they had been thrown into the rivers." Nowadays the railway is sued for damages if the salmon that was caught or the grouse that was shot in the furthest corner of Ross-shire on the Monday afternoon is not punctually delivered in Leadenhall or Billingsgate markets on the Wednesday morning.

Indeed it might fairly be argued that the Highland Company suffers in public estimation through the excess of its own virtue. The admirable service which has brought Wick, Thurso, and Portree within little more than twelve hours of Glasgow, often leads us to forget how deep is the gulf that yawns between them. We compare the Highland with the Caledonian and the North-Western, and we grumble if it falls short of our standard. The fairer comparison would be with some American or Australian "backwoods" line. The States have a significant railway term which is not in use in England. What we call a stopping or ordinary train, what the French call a *train omnibus*, the Americans describe as an "accommodation" train; in other words, their lines have been built for goods traffic, to afford an outlet to the markets of the great towns for the agricultural or mineral products of the neighbouring country. Passengers are almost an afterthought, and passenger trains are run rather for their accommodation as a favour than with an eye to profit. No American would expect from the Missouri and Pacific or the Wabash the same class of services that are given by the Pennsylvania or the New York Central. Out west, if they only get one passenger train in the twenty-four hours they make the best of it; if they get two, they are content; with three, they may consider themselves unusually well served; while as for speed, they are satisfied to label "express" anything that can reach an inclusive speed of 20 miles an hour. Tried by a somewhat similar standard, the Highland Company would be found to give most generous facilities.

To show how impossible it is to compare it on all-fours with an English line, let us set it side by side with a company of about the same nominal length of line, the Lancashire and Yorkshire. The Highland has 425 miles, all but 8 of them single line; the Lancashire and Yorkshire has 514, of which all but 22¼ are double or more than double. The capital in the former case is £4,700,000; in the latter it is just ten times as large. The English company's half-yearly income is over two millions, that of its Scotch contemporary a good deal under two hundred thousand. Not to elaborate the point too far, let it just be added that, to work its traffic, the Highland Company has 85 engines, while the Lancashire and Yorkshire has no less than 1050; and that, spite of all efforts to keep down the mileage, the Highland engines can only earn 4s. 4d. a mile, while the Lancashire and Yorkshire can secure on every mile an extra shilling. Southerners mostly see the Highland trains in August, when they are full enough in all conscience; they must have a very different look for at least eight months in the year. A railway newspaper chronicled a short time back that, no later in the season than the last week of September, the London Mail arrived at Oban, a much more frequented place than Wick or Strome Ferry, without a solitary passenger.

Let us see, however, what sort of service the Highland Company does in fact give. Tain, on the Dornoch Frith, is 638 miles from Euston, and has four through connections every day, averaging over 29 miles an hour throughout. To Strome, 677 miles from King's Cross, as well as to Wick, which is 768, the speed of the best train is well over 34. Compare this with points nearer home. No one will accuse the North-Western either of want of liberality or of bad management. Brinklow, Shilton, and Bulkington are three consecutive stations on the main line of the first railway company in the world. They lie just north of Rugby at an average distance of 91 miles from Euston. They have only five connections in the day, and the average speed is a little over 36.

The Highland Company is not unfrequently the object of severe reproaches from the inspecting officers of the Board of Trade for its sins both of omission and of commission. It ignores the

L

block system; it will have nothing to do with
train staff or train tablet, but works its traffic, as
does also its neighbour the Great North in most
parts, on the old-fashioned system of telegraphic
crossing orders; its facing points are often un-
provided with locking-bars, in some cases they
are not even interlocked with the signals. If an
attempt were made to open a new railway without
any or all of these modern improvements, the
Board of Trade would peremptorily refuse its
license. The line being opened, all the depart-
ment has hitherto been able to do is to protest,
and that it has done both frequently and vigo-
rously. Nor is this the only subject for its stric-
tures. The Board of Trade objects to pilot
engines "banking" up a train from behind.
They do not hesitate to use two "bank" engines
on the Highland when they want them. It
objects to mixed trains altogether. If it had its
own way, mixed trains would cease to exist, or at
least be reduced to one or two passenger carriages
attached, and always attached in front, to very
short goods trains, all of whose trucks would be
fitted with screw couplings. The Highland line
sets all these scruples at defiance. Most of its
trains are mixed, some of them very mixed
indeed, and the passenger carriages are always
in the rear. I came into Inverness not long
since from the North in a train of 35 goods trucks

followed by seven passenger coaches. I remarked to the guard that this was a good deal. "Long train, sir," was his reply; "why, we took in 50 trucks on this train last night, and I've seen me come in with 70."

Now let it be at once frankly admitted that all this elaborate apparatus of precaution does add somewhat to the safety of railway travelling. A tour on the Highland, while far from being as perilous as a run on the main line of the Paris and Lyons in the neighbourhood of Dijon, and still further from being as venturesome as a progress in a Russian Imperial special, must evidently be less absolutely safe than a journey on an express on a great English line. For all that, speaking as a frequent traveller who values his own life at least as highly as the President of the Board of Trade is likely to value other people's, I must confess that my own sympathies are very largely with the railway company. The public, as represented by the Board of Trade, are asking to eat their cake and have it too. After all, safety is only a question of degree. The Queen, many years back, wrote a letter expressing her desire that the safety of the meanest of her subjects should be cared for as her own. The thing is impossible. If pilot engines were sent in advance, if points were to be locked and bolted, goods traffic on the opposite line suspended, and so forth, every time each one of her subjects travelled, nine-tenths of them would have to stop at home entirely, and the trade of the kingdom would be absolutely paralysed. It needs no argument to show that, though all these precautions, which are specially taken for the sake of one exceptionally valuable life, do certainly reduce the risk of travelling to proportions even more homœopathic than usual, it would be absurd to employ them under ordinary circumstances.

To apply this argument to the case of the Highland. Unquestionably the signalling of the line might be made as elaborately perfect as it is on the Great Northern. It is only a question of money. Still, the money cost of a like reorganization was sufficiently serious not long since to determine the Great Northern, the Midland, and the Sheffield, to close the Winsford branch of the Cheshire Lines to passenger traffic altogether, rather than incur it. The Highland could scarcely adopt quite so drastic a course, but at least it would resolve, with competition to right, and competition to left, with the Caledonian tapping the west coast traffic at Oban, with the West Highland on the one side, and the Great North applying for a new line from Elgin to Inverness on the other, to refrain entirely from new extensions. To all appeals for branches to Ullapool or to Gairloch it would turn a deaf ear. As for the suppression of mixed trains, there can be no doubt that it would mean the withdrawal of a large portion of the passenger facilities now enjoyed. The passenger receipts are probably under 2s. a mile. Deduct the earnings of the expresses in summer, which must carry traffic worth ten times that amount, and the ordinary trains for the rest of the year probably do not average 1s. a mile; north of Helmsdale or west of Dingwall, perhaps not sixpence. And at this price passenger trains will not be run at all. If the people of Sutherland had the question fairly put before them, which would they choose? One train a day and no risk, or four times as many in return for a safety fractionally less absolute.

"Well, but," it will be said, "at least the passengers might be put in front, and engines need not be attached behind." Nor need they, if passengers are not in a hurry. But it requires no argument to show that, if a train has to stop at the top of an incline for the engine in front to uncouple and run back on to the opposite line, it takes five minutes more than if an engine behind is simply hitched off and drops back without the train stopping at all; and that means ten minutes' delay between Perth and Inverness. Again, you may put passenger coaches in front instead of behind the goods trucks, but in that case you must allow an extra seven or eight minutes at every station where shunting has to be done. For you must always begin by drawing up your passenger coaches at the platform, in order that passengers may get in and out; then you must put them across on to the other line, or into a siding; then come back to do the shunting, and when that is finished, go across once more to fetch the carriages. And seven or eight minutes at each of sixty stations between Perth and Wick means, in other words, seven or eight hours.

It is within my own knowledge that one of the great English companies was forced not long since, by the impossibility of complying with the Board of Trade requirements in this respect, to abandon mixed trains altogether on one of its country branches. It now works its goods and its passengers separate; and no doubt the Board of Trade is well satisfied that this should be so. But the extra expense, which was a flea-bite to the English company, would be ruination to the Highland. And if the Highland dividend was brought down to nothing, who would suffer most in the long run? The Highland shareholders, or the Highland customers? Is the game really worth all this candle? Put the question this way: How many men, having missed the last train, would hesitate to accept with gratitude a lift in the brake of a coal train? But to travel in a brake is unquestionably much more risky than in a first-class carriage. Or, again, was it a crime to risk the precious life of His Imperial Majesty the Shah of Persia over the roughly laid contractor's lines along the Manchester Ship Canal? And if not, why may we not be content on an out-of-the-way line with a practical instead of a theoretical standard of safety?

Apparently, however, the Highland will be compelled to conform to the theoretical standard ere long. Though, hitherto, the Board of Trade could only advise and request, henceforward, under the terms of the Railway Regulation Act, 1889, they are empowered to order any company to adopt block-working, to interlock its signals, and to use automatic brakes. In a circular recently issued they have given notice that every company will be required within a year or eighteen months to adopt all these precautions. In other words, speaking broadly, the lines in Ross and Caithness are to be brought up to the same standard of efficiency as is found on the main lines outside Euston or St. Pancras. Mixed trains are to be forbidden altogether, unless in exceptional circumstances, and in no case must the number of goods trucks exceed half the total number of vehicles on the train. Such is in plain terms the purport of the new circular, which adds, it should be said, a clause to the effect that the Board, before giving final orders, will be glad to hear from any company which has any objection to offer. As may be seen from what has gone before, to my mind, companies in the position of the Highland will have every objection. They will be able to point out that the new regulations, strictly enforced, would make their traffic unworkable, or workable only at a cost equal to or greater than the whole earnings of their railway.

It is easy to see the line which the Board of Trade reply will take. They will say, "Our concern is not with dividends, but with safety; public opinion demands these precautions in the interest of the public safety, our business is only to act as the mouthpiece of the public." And there will of course be a good deal of weight in the answer. But if the companies are referred to public opinion for a final decision, they will have to take care that the public has before it the materials for deciding fairly. It is not merely a case of safety *v.* dividends, but a case of setting up for universal adoption, at the risk of the withdrawal of a large portion of the facilities at present enjoyed, a theoretic standard of perfection as ridiculously out of place in remote districts as an improved wood-pavement would be in the back lane of the pettiest country village.*

---

* While justifying, broadly speaking, most of what the Highland has done and left undone, I yet think that the time has fully come when it ought to introduce either the staff

In one respect, and that a most important one, the Highland comes up to the highest standard. Whatever accidents may happen, they are not likely to be caused by any avoidable defect in engines or carriages. Of the new third-class carriages, Mr. Foxwell declares that "they are equal to the very newest of the wealthiest English companies," and his praise is not exaggerated. As for the engines, Crewe and Derby and Doncaster may equal, but cannot surpass in power of hauling heavy loads at high speeds, and can hardly equal in perfection of grooming, the iron steeds which are turned out by the Inverness stable. Perhaps when a loco-superintendent has only 85 engines, and can keep them all close under his own eye, he not only takes more pride in them, but can look after them better than when they are numbered by thousands and scattered in running sheds all over the country from Bournemouth to Carlisle. Among the peculiarities of the Highland engines may be noted the fact that the chimney is

---

or the tablet system and interlock all its facing points on the portion of the line between Perth and Inverness. There is another point I would like to notice, whether, namely, the introduction of what the French call *train-tramways*, light engines that is, with light cars attached, which are cheap to buy, cheap to work, and cheap as far as maintenance of permanent way is concerned, would not enable them to reduce the "mixed" mileage, at least in the more populous parts of the territory they serve.

double, and that in the front of the outer casing there are louvres, in order to counteract the effect of a high wind in checking the draught through the fire, a serious matter often in the wild Highland country. Another peculiarity, not visible externally however, is that some of the engines have their smoke-box roofed in, so to speak, with a grating a few inches below the foot of the chimney. This is found to arrest the sparks without tending, like spark-catchers on the top of the chimney, to check the draught.

A break-down on a railway is always a serious thing; but much more so when the line is single and there is no alternative route. So the Highland appliances for dealing with interruptions of traffic are of the most elaborate nature. At Inverness there is kept a steam break-down crane, which can work from either end, lift a weight of 15 tons, and swing it round in a circle with a radius of 25 feet, and can move itself, if necessary, while at work, from one place to another. The machine must have cost some thousands of pounds; but as the use of it may obviate the necessity of throwing three or four damaged carriages over an embankment in order to clear the line, the money may, no doubt, some day be proved to have been well spent. Attached to the truck on which the crane is mounted is a large and roomy van, whose interior looks a good deal like the model of an emigrant's hut. On every side are cupboards and lockers filled with provisions for the break-down gang. Here is a tin of coffee, there a cheese, in the corner yonder is a cask of biscuits. Everything down to the smallest detail is ready on board, and all is prepared for an instant start.

Accidents fortunately happen seldom, but snow blocks are almost of annual occurrence. Among the rolling stock enumerated in the half-yearly reports, there figure fifteen snow-ploughs. Many passengers coming up through the Pass of Killiecrankie, probably the finest railway view in Great Britain, will have observed a whole batch of them at Blair Athole. But far worse than the sheltered valleys of Perthshire are the bleak mosses of Caithness. Here in some parts the line is protected by a double row of snow fences.

At one point near Halkirk I noticed what looked like the roof of a shed only about three feet in height erected on the slope of the cutting through which the railway ran. That this structure had some connection with snow was obvious, but it was not easy to understand its manner of action. I have since learnt that it was a trial length of an "automatic snow-fence" patented by a Lancashire gentleman, Mr. W. L. Howie, and that its object is not merely to intercept the snow and keep it off the line, but to prevent snow-drifts from forming at all. Mr. Howie reasons as follows: drifts form in cuttings because the wind passes over the top, and allows the snow to fall through the still air to the ground below. A wind blowing along the surface of level ground drives the snow before it and prevents it from packing. Accordingly, to prevent snow-blocks from winds blowing across the line, against which alone provision need be made, he constructs a roof, whose ridge, so to speak, projects far enough out of the cutting to catch the wind and deflect it downwards along the slope of the bank. But the wind is only deflected; its force is not impaired, so it drives the snow before it across the rails and up the slope on the further side.

Unfortunately, so Mr. Howie thinks (the Highland Company perhaps would hardly be prepared to agree with him), there has been no snow to speak of in the far north for some years past, so the automatic snow-fence has scarcely had a fair trial. It is reported, however, that in slight falls the ground opposite it has been black while on either side it was white. But the idea has had a more serious trial than this. At Burghead, on the coast not far from Elgin, the Highland Company has been much troubled with drifting sand, and, in order to deal with it, they have erected a fence on Mr. Howie's principles, only made much deeper from top to bottom, as sand, being so much heavier than snow, needs a much sharper draught to blow it away. Here is one report as to the result, given by the company's assistant engineer :—" No sand opposite fence . . . the agent [station master] and leading surfaceman gave me their opinion that 40 men could not have kept the line clear on Friday night, and that, if the fence had not been there, there would have been at least four feet depth of sand over the rails."

If the fence can keep sand from accumulating on the line, it should surely be able to prevent snow-drifts also; but the inventor is naturally anxious to see it also tried in action with snow. The extreme north is not likely, one would think, to escape much longer, and possibly while these lines are passing through the press a furious snowstorm may be raging at Halkirk. But it is a far cry to Caithness, so leaving the country with its flagstone fences and its all-pervading fishiness, but its almost entire absence of railway trains, let us notice some special features of interest on the different lines.

V.—MINOR BUT MERITORIOUS FEATURES.

THE Prince of Wales every spring sends his hunters from Sandringham to Windsor for change of air; but in England, as a rule, less aristocratic animals have to do without an annual outing as best they may. Not so, however, in Scotland. In the fall of the year tens of thousands of the small Highland sheep from Skye and Stornoway are landed at Strome Ferry, and carried by the Highland Railway to the warm belt of rich country lying along the shores of the Moray Frith. There, to the great contentment of the Moray and Nairnshire farmer, they eat his turnips and manure his fields till spring comes round again, and they can return once more to their mountain pastures. The railway rate is sixpence per double mile for a truck-load of, say, fifty sheep; or, roughly, half a farthing per head. The Caledonian has a somewhat similar traffic, though on a smaller scale, from the Perthshire hills, and also *viâ* Oban from Argyll and the Western Islands to the low ground of Forfar and Kincardine, and even as far south as the Lothians.

But by no means all the Highland sheep provide themselves with return tickets. In or about the month of October each year there is an enormous exodus southwards. Dalwhinnie alone sometimes sends away 20,000 sheep within a few weeks, a large proportion of them going to the Carlisle market. Talking of markets, the July wool market at Inverness is of a somewhat remarkable character. Not a pound of wool is shown, for the best of reasons, namely, that it is still growing on the backs of the sheep perhaps a hundred miles away; but at this market the bulk of the Highland clip for the year is sold. Moreover, in many instances, the sheep themselves as well as their fleeces are sold in their absence, the price in either case being settled simply by the reputation of the flocks of the different breeders. To the lay mind it seems not a little strange that, if home-grown wool can be dealt with in this summary fashion, in the case of colonial wool for the London sales, it is found necessary, in order to permit of sampling every individual bale, to cart or lighter it all up from the docks to the neighbourhood of the sale-room in the heart of the City, and then cart it away again to the railway station on its road to the West Riding or the Stroud manufacturer.

This spring the sheep and cattle traffic from the West Highlands was largely swollen by exceptional circumstances. The grass on the East Coast farms grew so luxuriantly that the farmers were at a loss what to do with it, and bought great numbers of Highland cattle to eat it down. One great market for these latter is at the Muir of Ord, a point a few miles south of Dingwall, where the Skye line * diverges from the main road to the north. I was there one day last June, and was watching a mob of them being coaxed and driven into the railway trucks. All of a sudden up drove two long, low, narrow, covered carts, and from out of the carefully padded interior there stepped two yearling bulls of the black polled-Angus breed. They were beautiful little creatures, well worthy to take a prize at the Windsor Agricultural Show to which they were bound, and when their clothing was removed—for they were as tenderly cared for as any racehorse—their coats shone like satin; but by the side of those noble savages, the Highland cattle, with their straight sharp horns and their bright eyes gleaming through the shaggy masses of red hair, they looked about as much out of place

* The Skye line is the usual name for the branch which runs across Ross-shire from Dingwall to Strome Ferry. It is of course named—on the same principle which induced the sanguine promoters of the railway from Aberystwith to Pencader to christen their road the "Manchester and Milford"—because it is the natural route to the Island of Skye. But the first time I heard it, having no opportunity of seeing the spelling, I thought it was a mere nick-name, analogous to the Michigan "Air" line, or the "Nickel Plate" Railway.

as a couple of palefaces in evening dress would have looked in the midst of a party of Indian braves.

To make up for the unusually large cattle traffic there was a considerable falling off in the West Highland herring fishery. In 1888 the weight of fish caught was over 7000 tons; last spring the amount was but little over 4000. In 1888 steam carriers, which took the fish as far south as Fleetwood, entered for the first time into competition with Strome Ferry and Oban, and as there was plenty of fish for all three routes, they did well enough; but last spring their owners were probably forced to the reluctant conclusion that, taking the rough with the smooth, railway rates may not be so much too high after all. To add to the Fleetwood association's disappointment, after their boats had been taken off, the fish that according to all precedent ought to have come to be caught in May and June, did come later on in September and October; and the fish trucks, that in the earlier months were standing idle by hundreds at Strome Ferry, then had a busy enough time of it.

Fish and cattle traffic not only comes in rushes and by fits and starts, but also, needless to say, must be worked, when it does come, with the utmost promptitude. The endeavour to do so over long stretches of single line without delaying the rest of the traffic has given rise to one or two interesting developments of what is probably the most perfect method of single-line working, that which is known as Tyer's Electric Tablet System. Elsewhere* I have described that system fully, and pointed out its superiority over the ordinary method of staff and ticket. Suffice it here to say that the line is divided into sections; that to every section there is assigned a set of metal tablets with the name of the section engraved upon them; and that no train is permitted to pass over any section unless one of the corresponding tablets is in the driver's possession. When the section is unoccupied, the whole of the tablets, and when a train is in it, all except the one in the driver's possession, are kept in boxes at either end, which are securely locked by an electric current. Now the Callander and Oban line mounts a steep incline for the first two miles after leaving Oban, and then runs down an equally abrupt incline on the further side, to Connal Ferry station, four miles away, where the tablet is exchanged for one bearing the name of the succeeding, Connal Ferry to Taynuilt, section. Up the incline the trains often need the assistance of a "bank" engine, which is detached at the top, and returns by itself—or to use the technical phrase, "light"—to Oban. There would, therefore, be a possibility that a down train, starting from Connal Ferry as soon as the up train had passed, might

* 'Railways of England,' p. 394.

catch this engine up and run into it before it got back home. To obviate this risk, there has been introduced, in addition to the tablet, which is carried in the ordinary way by the train engine, a staff not unlike a small policeman's truncheon, which is given to the driver of the "bank" engine. This staff forms a part of the electric lock which closes the tablet-boxes, and the result is therefore that, till the "bank" engine has got back to Oban, and returned its staff to the box at that end, it is impossible for the signalman at Connal Ferry to get a tablet out of his box, so as to send forward a down train which may be waiting there. Another and more amusing, except perhaps for the stationmasters, if less ingenious, modification is this. A fish or cattle boat may arrive at Oban after the line is closed for the night, and it may be desirable to send forward its cargo immediately. Arrangements have therefore been made by which the act of closing and locking the door of the booking office at intermediate stations diverts an electric circuit through a bell placed in the station-master's bedroom, a current can therefore at any moment be sent along the line, which will ring the bells and warn the station-masters to get up and make the necessary arrangements for working the coming train.

One of the chief disadvantages of the tablet system is found in the fact that it is necessary to stop or at least to slacken speed at the various stations to exchange tablets. It is true that on some lines, in order that they may be exchanged the more speedily, the tablets are hung on wire rings of perhaps a foot in diameter, through which driver and signalman respectively thrust their arms as the train runs by. But this plan is certainly not free from risk. I have never heard of any accident actually happening, but it is at least conceivable that a man might be knocked down insensible by a disc of metal a couple of pounds in weight striking him on the head, that his arm might almost be pulled out of the socket, or even that he might be dragged under the wheels of the train. On the Great North of Scotland, where the tablet system is in use on the newly opened Buckie Extension, the locomotive superintendent has accordingly devoted much time and thought to the construction of an apparatus which should exchange tablets automatically, much in the same fashion as the travelling post-office apparatus exchanges mailbags. I had the opportunity of seeing the new invention at work on the second day of its performance in public some time last May, and being on the engine could watch its action closely. Everything worked without a hitch, even the driver expressed his approval—and it is no small triumph to win the approval of an engine-driver to new-fangled innovations—and I have since heard that six months' experience has only confirmed the first impressions.

Briefly, the apparatus consists of an iron post some five feet in height, standing at one end of the platform, just far enough back from the rails to clear in safety the engine and carriages of a passing train. From the side of the engine, a little above the foot-plate, a corresponding arm, which can be drawn back, and even altogether removed when not in use, projects level with the top of the platform post. Both post and arm have sticking out on either side of them what looks something like a pair of exaggerated tuning-forks, and the two pairs of course correspond with one another except that their action is reversed. For the pair fixed on the post has strong jaws facing the approaching train to receive and grasp firmly the tablet which it brings, while the jaws on the other side are much more lightly constructed, and hold but loosely the tablet which the train will have to pick up. The arm on the engine, on the other hand, has for the same reason the jaws in front strong, while those behind are weak. Imagine then a train approaching the station. A tablet, enclosed in a square envelope of stout india-rubber, is placed both by engine-driver and signalman in the weak, that is the delivery, fork. The engine reaches the post, its projecting arm sweeps over the top, a sharp click is heard, the delivery forks are empty while the two receiving forks have each safely caught their tablet, which a moment later is extracted from their tightly clenched jaws by the help of a strong brass disgorger. As I saw the apparatus at work, when everything was new and the operators unfamiliar with their duties, the speed of the train was reduced on each occasion to some 15 to 20 miles an hour. But now that further experience has been gained, the exchange is daily made at what is practically full speed. One point more must just be added. Mr. Manson has refused to patent his invention, and it may be adopted freely by any company that wishes to do so. No pecuniary interests of his own, so he quietly replied when I asked the reason, should delay for one hour the introduction of an apparatus which he hoped would tend to protect railway servants from risk of injury in the discharge of their duties.

The question of single-line working naturally recalls us to the Ayrshire and Wigtownshire, with its thirty miles of line all single, of which mention was made in the first chapter. This plucky little company, which may be taken as the single exception proving the rule that in Scotland the small undertakings have all been 'amalgamated into fair-sized systems, has a curious history. Its *raison d'être* was the construction of a line from Girvan in South Ayrshire, the terminus of the Glasgow and South Western, to Challoch, where a junction was made with the Portpatrick and Wigtownshire, so affording direct access from Glasgow to Stranraer and Portpatrick. The line was duly made, but at the cost of £600,000, a sum ridiculously disproportionate not only to the necessary expense of construction but also to the possible returns of the traffic. For though the country at either end is fertile enough, the Ayrshire and Wigtownshire itself runs through a desert. Mile after mile there is scarcely a sign of life, unless it be the wooden labels hung at intervals along the telegraph wires to give notice to the grouse not to fly too high. If the line was to live at all, it would have to exist not by local but by through traffic. And that was hardly to be obtained at prices which would more than pay for working expenses over so heavy a road.

From the very first the line was in difficulties. It was worked by the Glasgow and South Western, and the South Western gave it a service which in its proprietors' opinion only starved the line, but which the South Western in their turn declared could not be given by them except at a loss. More than once the line was closed altogether. Finally the Court of Session ordered it to be sold out and out for what it would fetch. The only railway in the neighbourhood, except the South Western itself, is the Wigtownshire and Portpatrick, which is the joint property of the South Western, the Midland, the Caledonian, and the North Western. The joint board agreed not to bid, and then it was supposed that the South Western would be able to buy the line almost at its own price. How much exactly it offered, I cannot say. I was told £150,000 on authority which I should have supposed conclusive, had I not been assured by another gentleman who ought to have been equally well informed that the bid was only £100,000. Be that as it may, to everybody's surprise, a private syndicate of London capitalists bid £155,000, got the line at the price, and what is more, determined to work it themselves. From the energy with which they have undertaken their task, it is even possible that, with so small a capital, they may be able to work it at a fair profit. In that case, the South Western, which sooner or later is almost certain to have to buy the line, will need to offer a considerable advance on £150,000.

Meanwhile the task is unquestionably an uphill one. It is true that Portpatrick is a harbour with a history, as it was in former times the route by which the mails were sent to Ireland; and hereafter perhaps, if, after finishing the Channel Tunnel and his improved Eiffel Tower, Sir Edward Watkin has time to turn his attention to the subject, it may rise to fame as the starting-point of the new Irish Tunnel to Donaghadee; but at the present moment it is little better than a fishing village. In fact the whole place struck me, when I saw it, as very much like a large-scale model. There was a toy harbour with a toy breakwater in front, with the stump of a toy lighthouse upon it. Close beside, the walls of a deserted cottage might have been made by a very slight stretch of imagination to do duty for the ruins of a miniature castle; while, to complete the illusion, the postman, who came to the station to fetch Her Majesty's mails, was a small boy who wheeled away one tiny mail-bag on a child's go-cart.

Stranraer of course is on a different scale from this, and is a place with a considerable Irish trade. At the present moment a new steamer for the cross-channel service to Larne is being built by Denny of Dumbarton, which is to be not unlike the fine new Ostend boats, and is to maintain a speed of eighteen knots an hour. But the traffic of the Stranraer route is to the East of Scotland and to England, in fact to anywhere rather than to Glasgow. From Glasgow to Belfast the goods traffic naturally goes by sea throughout, and for the portion which does come to Stranraer both the Glasgow and South Western and the Caledonian have roads of their own, though longer, round by Dumfries; while passengers prefer to join the boats which sail from Ardrossan or Greenock, rather than take a long and tedious railway journey, followed by a sea passage and then a second change into a train. Moreover, the boats leave Stranraer early in the morning to suit the arrival of the London night-mails, so that Glasgow passengers would need to reach Stranraer over-night, for an attempt that has more than once been made to start an express about 6 A.M. from Glasgow has had to be abandoned for lack of support. Last summer Messrs. Burns, the steamship owners who have monopolized the Glasgow Belfast route for more than half a century, put on a splendid new steamer of 4000 horse-power specially for passenger traffic, by which it was possible, leaving Glasgow at 8 in the morning, to be in Belfast by 1.45 P.M., and on the return journey, leaving Belfast at 3 P.M., to reach Glasgow at 9.40.* So the natural result is that, for all its energy, the little Ayrshire and Wigtownshire cannot do much with the through Irish traffic.

* The *Cobra* was a fine vessel, but she did not quite come up to the specified requirements. So Messrs. Burns refused to accept her, except as a temporary stop-gap, and the Fairfield yard has got to try its hand again. It is reported that the new vessel next summer will probably sail not from Gourock but from Ardrossan. And it is worth mention, as a sample of the keenness of Scotch competition, that, though both the South Western and the Caledonian have railway piers at Ardrossan, it is understood that the boat will be run in connection with a Caledonian train service, because from the pier of this latter company a vessel can steam straight away, while in the case of the South Western it is necessary for her to turn round.

Working for a Dividend. 171

This would be bad enough, but worse remains behind. There is a considerable amount of agricultural produce, cheese more especially, sent from the neighbourhood of Stranraer to the Glasgow market. Of this, if it were a case of railway competition only, the Ayrshire and Wigtownshire ought to get a fair share. But here the coasting steamers step in and carry off the traffic by offering prices which a railway, and especially one working over heavy gradients, cannot afford to take. Considering all these disadvantages the energy and enterprise which the little line displays is worthy of high commendation. It has recently bought some excellent new carriages, and its best train runs from Dunragit to Girvan, with four intermediate stops and a long "set-back" into Girvan station, 32 miles in the level hour. Travelling by this train the other day, I had a good opportunity of seeing how hard a commercial undertaking will work for a dividend. A farmer was very anxious to send a horse by it to a station at which the train was not booked to stop. It was pointed out to him that to take the horse-box would delay the train at least five minutes, as the engine would have to draw it away on to the other line, and then come back and couple up to the carriages. But the man persisted in urging his request. So finally the horse-box was attached at the tail of the train, a second brake-van being placed behind it for safety's sake, and the one horse and the two vehicles were hauled off to New Luce and there detached. The farmer was satisfied, and the Ayrshire and the Wigtownshire was richer by perhaps five shillings. If every crown is as hardly earned, there should not be many people to grudge the new proprietors their modest 1¼ per cent. of dividend. Let those who look forward to a millennium of State-owned railways—a body which seems to be increasing in numbers in Great Britain at present, though curiously enough in Germany, after a decade's experience of State-ownership, the trend of public opinion is all the other way—say whether Government officials would be likely to give their subjects equal facilities.

In the first of the magazine articles upon which this book is based it was stated that "in universal and ubiquitous competition is to be found the keynote of the Scotch railway system." This statement has since been taken by one of the Scotch chairmen as the text of his discourse at the half-yearly meeting of his shareholders, so perhaps it may now be considered as having received an official *imprimatur*. From that competition there flow naturally two results. On the one hand the companies are driven to do their utmost to economize in working their traffic. The average proportion of the gross earnings absorbed in working expenses is only about 47 per cent. in

Scotland as against something like 52 per cent. in England. One instance in which economy has been effected that must be patent to every traveller in Scotland, is to be found in the abolition of second-class. Second-class carriages still run all over the Highland line, and on the East Coast and West Coast through trains to and from England. But elsewhere they have practically ceased to exist. A year or two back they disappeared from the Edinburgh and Glasgow expresses; last summer they were given up on the "coast" trains from Glasgow. The Great North has, it is true, not abandoned second-class, but that is for the best possible reason—it never had any. We have lately been told on good authority that Sir James Allport, though he only succeeded in abolishing second-class on the Midland in 1875, urged upon the Sheffield board the propriety of adopting such a policy as far back as 1850. Whether it was from Sir James that the Great North learnt wisdom, probably no one now alive can say, but the fact is certain that the line has never possessed any second-class carriages.

Whether, however, their former habit of charging what practically were second-class fares for ordinary third-class accommodation was an improvement on the usual practice is a different question. From a "Bradshaw" only ten years old one can see that from Aberdeen to Banff, 65 miles, the first-class fare was 10s., third-class 7s. 2d., "government" 4s. 9½d.; to Boat of Garten, 101 miles, the charges were 17s. 6d., 12s. 6d., and 8s. 5d. respectively. In those days there was only one "government" train each way in the 24 hours, and as it took 7 hours and 20 minutes over its 100 miles, it did not much exceed its parliamentary minimum of 12 miles an hour. Needless to say, nowadays, almost all over the kingdom—the most conspicuous and least justifiable exception with which I am acquainted is to be found on the Wye Valley section of the Great Western system—" parliamentary" and "third-class" are convertible terms, and any passenger who knows the distance he is going to travel knows, not always the minimum, but certainly the maximum number of pence he will have to pay.

But to come back to the abolition of second-class, for my own part I can scarcely doubt that the Scotch companies have done wisely. No doubt they have sacrificed a portion of the fares of the passengers who formerly went second and now travel third, but in return they have done a good deal to simplify and to lighten their trains. And this is a very serious matter. The question is often discussed as though it were merely one of dividing a train into two or three subdivisions. In fact a main line train is as a rule composed of portions for, say, four different places, and on each portion the company is expected to provide accommodation for ordinary passengers, for smokers, and latterly also for ladies, of all three classes. Thirty-six subdivisions in all, or a good long train, even if one compartment apiece was all that was required. Strike out second-class, and you reduce your possible subdivision at one blow from thirty-six to twenty-four.

It may be said: Why not then abolish first-class also, for it pays, if Mr. Findlay's figures may be relied on, even worse than second? The answer is here, not that it is theoretically wrong, but that it is practically impossible. It would be not a reform but a revolution, and no company dare lead the way. The great iron-masters, or coal-owners, or manufacturers, who found themselves suddenly compelled to travel third-class, would avenge themselves for the discomfort by sending tens of thousands of pounds' worth of traffic by the rival line. Besides, as long as society in Great Britain is organized as it is, it must be admitted that most people would find it incongruous, if Lord Salisbury for instance had to travel between King's Cross and Hatfield in a third-class compartment. With second-class passengers there are no such difficulties. They are neither distinguished nor influential, and as long as compartments—third as well as first—are reserved for ladies travelling alone, the only class likely to be in any way inconvenienced by the change is amply protected.

The other result of competition may be said to be the concession of advantages and facilities even beyond those to which we are accustomed on the most liberal lines in England. For instance, to meet the steamboat competition, passengers are carried every Tuesday and Friday—not in summer only, but all the year round—from Edinburgh to Aberdeen, 160 miles, for *7s. 6d.* Over a large part of the country return tickets are issued every Saturday at very little more than single fares for the double journey. The minimum time for which an ordinary return ticket is available is one month, very frequently six months are allowed. From Glasgow to the north the ordinary return fare is only a single fare and a quarter. Then for the southern part of the country, where return fares are calculated on the basis of a fare and a half, there is the peculiarly Scotch institution of "Guest tickets." Holders of season-tickets, say between Glasgow and Largs or Moffat, can obtain batches of return tickets for the use of their families or friends coming to stay with them at a single fare and a quarter.

Here are some samples of liberal treatment within my own personal knowledge. A gentleman the other day took a monthly season-ticket from Glasgow to the sea-side. Two days after the ticket was issued he was taken ill, and it was over three weeks before he was able to return to business. He stated the fact to the company, which at once consented to cancel the ticket, and hand him back the money less the ordinary return fare for the two days on which it had actually been used. Some years since, coming down from England by the night-mail, a party of three, of whom I was one, missed the connection from Kilmarnock to Ayr, owing to the unpunctuality not of the Scotch but of the English company; and consequently we reached our destination about two hours late. More out of curiosity to see what he would say than for any other reason, I wrote to the general manager of the Glasgow and South Western, at that time an entire stranger to me, and laid my grievance before him. Next day a reply was despatched, expressing regret that the station-master at Kilmarnock had not sent us forward "special" at once, and stating that orders had been given that this course should always be adopted in future. It ought to be added that in this instance (as also in the two following) the traffic is entirely non-competitive.

As for children, the liberality with which they are treated is almost ridiculous. I remember a gentleman going with his wife, two nurses, and six children, ranging in age from twelve down to three, to spend the day at a place twenty miles away

With the full approval of the responsible officials, though the company had a right to charge for seven, he took four tickets for the entire party. Again, a boy of fourteen at school in Edinburgh came down to stop from Saturday to Monday with his people at their house in the country, some sixty miles away. He tendered half a guest-ticket to the collector, but it was promptly returned, with the remark that his father was a season-ticket holder and that was quite sufficient. School children indeed make use of the railway in Scotland to a much larger extent than is the case in England. It is impossible not to notice the numbers of them who come into the country towns every morning and go back again to their homes in the afternoon. No doubt, however, this is due to the Scotch preference of a day-school over a boarding-school education, quite as much as to the liberality of the railway companies.

In one respect Scotland is distinctly in advance of England. Two of the leading companies have begun to experiment in heating their carriages by methods less primitive than the universal English hot-water tin. On the Glasgow and South Western the waste heat from the roof-lamps of the carriages is the agent employed. Above the flame of the lamp is fixed a miniature wrought-iron boiler, connected by two small pipes with a reservoir placed below the seat. The hot water from the boiler is forced down into the reservoir, whence it drives out the cooler water before it, and sends it up to the roof to supply its place. In fact, with the exception that in this instance the kitchen fire is placed, after the fashion now usually adopted in the most luxurious *ménages*, on the top floor, the system is merely that which is adopted for the supply of hot water in every modern house. The system in use on the Caledonian makes use on the other hand of the waste steam of the engine —or rather of so much of it as escapes from the cylinder of the Westinghouse brake-pump. Iron pipes, connected between the coaches by pieces of old worn-out india-rubber brake-hose, run from end to end of the train. In each compartment there is, under the seat and connected with the train pipe, a pipe four inches in diameter which serves as a radiator. To allow the water, as it condenses, to escape, a tiny hole is made in the bottom of the bend of each of the india-rubber connections. This system has now been in use for some time on several of the Glasgow suburban trains, and the only objection I have heard made to it is, that passengers ought to have the power of shutting off the steam when they please, as the carriage often gets unpleasantly hot.

The Caledonian locomotive and carriage works at St. Rollox are, however, busied with matters much more serious than carriage heating. Merely as engineering shops they are well worth a visit. They are not perhaps quite the finest belonging to any railway company in Great Britain—that proud position probably belongs to the still newer shops of the Lancashire and Yorkshire at Horwich —and of course they are by no means the largest ; but compared to places such as Crewe or Doncaster, which consist of the gradual accretions of well-nigh half a century, their spaciousness and general convenience is instantly visible. Strangely enough, the most famous Caledonian engine—some people might say the most famous engine at present running in Great Britain—the wonderful No. 123, which, week in, week out, for nearly two years, has taken the Carlisle-Edinburgh express up the Beattock "bank," with its gradient of 1 in 75 or 80 for 10 miles, at a speed which most lines would term express along a dead level—was not built at St. Rollox at all, but by the well-known private firm of Neilson, though of course to the designs of the Caledonian locomotive superintendent. Hitherto, moreover, the type has not been repeated, and No. 123, with her 7-foot single drivers, remains so far alone in her class. Mr. Drummond's new engines are all "4-coupled ;" but if he expects them to surpass the performance of their predecessor, he must be an unusually sanguine man.

I was behind her the first time that the West Coast went from London to Edinburgh in 8 hours

She was booked to cover the 100¼ miles from Carlisle in 112 minutes, and the railway servants themselves declared that the thing was impossible. But she did it in 104, and went up the 10 miles from Beattock Station to Beattock Summit in 14 minutes, spite of a check at the signal half-way up which brought our speed down to some 15 miles an hour. Three days later, according to some most careful observations which have been furnished to me by a gentleman who went down for the purpose of recording the speed, the run was made from start to finish in 102 minutes 33 seconds. At the top of the incline, after 6 miles of 1 in 75, the train was still going at the rate of 37 miles an hour. On both days the load was the same, between 75 and 80 tons. Another day, long after the excitement of the great "Race" was over, and when the Edinburgh and Glasgow carriages were worked once more on the same train, I was on the footplate, when she took a train of ten coaches for several miles on end at an average speed of 65 miles an hour, not down hill but along the level. On this occasion we stopped at the foot of the incline for a "pilot," and including this stop, the 10 miles took 15 minutes. Now that the respective possibilities of West Coast and East Coast routes are being somewhat keenly canvassed, it is perhaps worth while to point out that the disadvantage to the West Coast caused by the existence of this climb of 1000 feet, as compared with a similar distance over perfectly level line, cannot at the outside be estimated at more than 5 minutes. A disadvantage it is, and must remain unquestionably, but not a disadvantage so overpowering that it cannot be abundantly compensated elsewhere in the course of a run of 400 or 500 miles.*

There are already a good many of the new type of express engine, with 4-coupled 6 feet 6 inches driving-wheels and a 4-wheeled bogie in front, at work on the line, and they are constantly put to most severe tests; for no line, take it for all in all, hauls as heavy trains over as bad a road at higher speed than does the Caledonian. Not only their power but their endurance is constantly tested, for it has latterly become an everyday thing for the same engine to run right through, for the whole

---

* Sir John Fowler's extraordinary appeal to the Board of Trade, to order the West Coast to throw up the sponge and surrender at discretion to their Forth Bridge rivals, makes it only fair to add that even on the East Coast it is not all plain sailing. The speed over the Tay Bridge is limited at present to 25 miles an hour. If this precaution is thought right now, will it become unnecessary next summer? Again, will trains run over the Forth Bridge at full speed from the first? If not, here we have the Beattock bank fully compensated for already. If they do, does Sir John Fowler think that it will be the duty of the West Coast officials to invoke the aid of the Board of Trade to protect East Coast passengers from the terrible risk that they will be unwittingly incurring?

240 miles, between Aberdeen and Carlisle. So much so indeed, that recently this was done even in the case of the Queen's special. When I was last at St. Rollox, some six months back, a batch of six of these engines, with 18-inch cylinders and 26-inch stroke, was under construction. They were alike in every particular except this, that two were to work at a boiler pressure of 150 lbs., two at 175 lbs., and two at 200 lbs.—this last a pressure that has never hitherto, as far as I am aware, been adopted for locomotives.* For Mr. Drummond, who is no believer in "compounds," shares with Mr. Johnson of the Midland the opinion, that the unquestioned economy of fuel shown by engines of this type is due not to the principle of compounding, but to the higher steam-pressure at which they are usually worked. Another novel feature which they possess is a sanding apparatus, worked not by steam, which is said to be liable to condense and so clog the pipes, but by a jet of compressed air from the Westinghouse pump. These engines have also exceptionally large steam-ports, that so the back-pressure of the escaping steam, which at extreme speeds mounts up very rapidly till it finally absorbs almost the whole power of the engine, may be reduced to a minimum.

* Never, at least, in this country. Some of the compounds exhibited last year at Paris are constructed to work at about 220 lbs. pressure.

They have just left the shops within the last month or two, and those who are interested in locomotive progress will watch their future performances with interest. If there are not abundant opportunities of doing so in the course of the coming summer, at least the Scotch public will be much disappointed of their present expectations.

Compressed air is turned to another use at St. Rollox, namely, to help the men in the foundry to make the moulds for their castings. By the force of compressed air the two sides of a casting-box are brought together in a fraction of the time that was needed under the old hand system; while the turning of a tap on a flexible pipe from the air reservoir sends all the particles of loose sand away in an instant and spares the moulder much unnecessary puffing and blowing.

Adjoining the locomotive shops there is an establishment which, though its like must exist on every railway, has not hitherto, as far as I am aware, won for itself a place in railway literature, and that is the grease factory. The importance of this establishment is perhaps hardly what it was a few years back, for on passenger carriages grease is rapidly being superseded by oil; for goods and mineral trucks, however, it is still indispensable. The reason for the difference depends on the difference of the work required. Oil is a more perfect lubricant than grease, and therefore renders the friction less when the train is actually running. On the other hand, it is much thinner and less viscous, so that, when the wheel is at rest, it is squeezed out and allows the axle-box to come down hard upon the axle, while grease would have left a film between. In other words, with grease the friction at the first start is much less. Now goods trucks start and stop much oftener than passenger carriages; they stand still for a much longer time; and what is still more important, a goods engine is habitually loaded to its full power, and therefore has as much as it can do to set its train in motion. Consequently for goods trucks grease still holds the field, and for the use of its 45,000 goods trucks the Caledonian railway manufactures some 600 or 700 tons of grease per annum.

The ingredients consist of palm-oil, soap, soda, tallow, and a small quantity of an extremely fluid white oil which looks not unlike the finest castor-oil. They are turned in by barrow-loads at a time into a huge boiler. This boiler is jacketed with steam, and the inner lining is perforated, so that jets of live steam can be admitted all round. More water is added to bring the mixture to the proper consistency—thicker or thinner according to the weather and the time of year—and then the whole is made to boil freely, after which it is drawn off into shallow vats and left for a day or two, to cool and harden. Finally it is dug out, placed in casks, and sent away down the line to the different goods and mineral depots.

It was mentioned above that the Caledonian is the owner of 45,000 trucks. Perhaps it would not be wrong to imagine that its shareholders have no reason to rejoice in the fact. Theoretically there can be no question that the railway companies ought to own the trucks which work over their line. The system of private ownership of railway waggons, says the great American authority, Professor Hadley, " gives to English freight trains a disreputable appearance which contrasts almost ludicrously with the solid excellence of the line and buildings. An uninstructed observer might readily suppose that the companies had spent all their money on the permanent way, and having nothing left for equipment, were tottering on the verge of hopeless bankruptcy." Mr. Hadley further declares, and it would be difficult to contradict him, that the system "is inconvenient to both railroads and shippers. The shippers complain of damage and detention of cars ; the railways complain of waste of space and power ; and both parties have good ground for their complaints." He might have added that it is highly dangerous to the public safety. Spite of inspection and repairs as frequent and as thorough as railway companies, with competitors on either side hungering for their traffic, dare to enforce, one or two private traders will always persist in sending over the railway waggons, which, if they had been the property of the railway company, would have found their way to the scrap-heap years before. Ninety-nine times when these waggons break down no harm is done, except that the line is blocked and the traffic disorganized, but the hundredth time the break-down comes when a passenger train is passing on the opposite line, and a terrible disaster is the natural result.

Professor Hadley ascribes the long continuance of this indefensible system to "English conservatism," and "the inertia of English business habits." This perhaps is scarcely an adequate explanation. The evil—and it must be remembered that, in the case of a large and prosperous coal or iron company working its trucks over the line of a small, poverty-stricken railway company, it is not an evil at all—can only be stopped by general and compulsory legislation. No single railway dare promote a Bill to banish private waggons off its line altogether. The thing must be done universally or not at all. It is not enough merely to offer to buy up the traders' waggons. This the Midland set to work to do some ten years back and allocated a million pounds of capital to the operation. But the result has not been over-encouraging. They have bought a great many, and, if they were not to offend their customers, they had sometimes not to be too critical about the prices. Then they had to spend almost as much as would have built new waggons in putting the old ones into thorough repair. The Caledonian, which followed in the Midland footsteps, has had a yet more disappointing experience. The traders, having disposed of their old waggons at a very satisfactory price, forthwith proceeded to spend the money in the purchase of new ones; so that the day when the company will own and be responsible for all the stock which runs on its line seems to be just as far off as ever.

There is another charge, which is yet more frequently brought by American writers against our railway management in this country, and that is the size of our goods waggons. If they held 30 tons as in America, instead of 5 or 10 as is the custom here (so we have been constantly assured of late in railway newspapers by a gentleman who appears to hold a brief for the American system), we should be able to work our traffic for many millions less per annum than is spent at present. It may be so, but, before the change is made, it might be well that we should be informed how it is proposed to manipulate a truck 36 feet long built with steel tubular framing—some people have been rude enough to describe it as gas-piping— when it comes to hoisting it on board a vessel, as is the custom in Glasgow, in order to tip its contents straight into the hold. At St. Rollox, at least, the feat is believed to be impossible. Not that they are by any means wedded to the old idea of a four-wheeled truck. On the contrary they have built a considerable number of trucks of a much larger size. These run on six wheels, two of which are fixed to the frame in the middle, while the remaining pairs are on bogies at either end. The weight is something under 10 tons, the capacity about 15 tons, and the length 26 feet. Beyond this size, say the Caledonian authorities, it is not profitable to go under our insular conditions.

But we have dwelt perhaps too much on Caledonian specialities. Let it, however, be said in excuse, that a writer can only describe what he has the opportunity of describing; and, be the fault whose it may, I have seen more which merits description on the Caledonian system than on that of its great rival. Still, before this sketch is brought to a close, we must note one most interesting point on the North British railway, an extremely ingenious method of electric lighting. As already mentioned, that company has a line, known as the City and District, running underground across the heart of Glasgow. Some of the trains on it start from Edinburgh and work right through as far as Helensburgh. For ten minutes they are in darkness, for the rest of the three hours in the open day. The carriages cannot be left unlighted for the ten minutes; on the other hand, it seems a gratuitous waste to keep lamps burning all the time. Here is the system which has been devised in order to comply economically with these conditions.

Through each of the three Glasgow tunnels there is laid a centre rail, raised up $4\frac{1}{4}$ inches above the ordinary metals and insulated from contact with the ground. This rail is kept charged with electricity, generated by the dynamos used for the lighting of the Queen Street station, which stands over the top of the underground railway. Underneath each carriage is an iron pulley with a spring to keep it in contact with the rail. Originally wire brushes were used instead of pulleys, but the points of the wires were fused so rapidly that this had to be abandoned. The current is led from the pulley through incandescent roof-lamps, then passes down the wheels, and so returns along the ordinary rails. There are two lamps in each compartment; in the first-class compartments both are lit, in the third they are so arranged that, though only one is lighted, if the one is broken or removed —and two or three are stolen every week—the other is automatically thrown into circuit. It should be added that the centre rail slopes up at either end very gradually from the ground to its full height, to avoid a sudden jerk to an advancing

The Prospects of the Future. 191

train, and that the cost, allowing for interest, depreciation, &c., works out to about one penny per hour for each lamp actually burning. In practice, they are found to burn on an average about one hour per diem. The advantages of the system are obvious. Each carriage is independent. Electrically lighted and oil-lighted carriages can be mixed up together in the same train. The electric lamps can at any moment be taken out and ordinary lamps substituted. And last, but by no means least, neither guard nor driver—both of whom have usually quite enough to do as it is—need to pay the smallest attention to the matter.

Here these notes end. Having sketched what seems of most general interest on the Scotch Railways as they are to-day, it only remains for the writer to add that, to judge by present indications, if a new edition should be called for twelve months hence, it is highly probable that, to meet the altered circumstances, a large portion of the book will have to be re-written.

INDEX.

A.

ABBOTSFORD, 109
Aberdeen, 123; granite quarries, 138, 139; cattle-raising, 139
Abergeldie Castle, 123
Aberlour, 134
Accidents, 155
Accommodation — Perth, 65; Aberdeen, 65; *Trains*, 143
Alford, 121
Allport, Sir James, 173
Amalgamation — Glasgow and S.W. with N. British, 4, 5, 28, 75, 80, 81
—— original North British, 40
—— Scottish, Central, and Scottish North-Eastern, 67
—— schemes, earlier failures of, 76
Anderson, James, C.E., 51
Anecdotes — The horse "Dragon," 15; horse passenger, 17; R. Smith's daughter, 104; cock-pheasant, 110; Napoleon's cutlet, 111; mushrooms, 114, 115; the unregenerate Great North; a fish special, 131; kerb-stones, 139; Mr. Andrew Wright, 139; cattle driving, 139; impenitent sinner, 147; working for a dividend, 171; liberality to customers, 176–8
Annandale, 44
Ardrossan Canal, the, 26
—— steamers to Belfast, 169
Arrol, Mr., 52
Aviemore, 61, 74, 122
Ayrshire and Wigtownshire Rly., 41, 166, 167; Irish traffic, 170

B.

BAIRDS of Gartsherrie, 70
Baker, Mr., 52
Ballachulish, 73
Ballater, 123
Ballochney Rly., 16, 17
Balmoral Castle, 123
"Bank" Engine, 162
—— holiday, 1854, 81
Beattock bridge,
"Bank," 30–32, 180–182
"Beef-factory," 139
Berwick to Edinburgh on a cattle train, 111
Blondin, a, 158
Boat of Garten, 133

O

Bo'ness, 19
Bouch, Sir Thomas, 52
Braemar, 122
Bridge of Earn, 54
Buchan Rly., 123
Buckie Extension Rly., 128; signalling, 164
Bulls, Angus, 160
Burghead, 156
Burns, *Messrs.*, 170

C.

CAIRNGORMS, the, 122
Caledonian Rly., 3; Clydesdale Junction, 5; leading Glasgow Rly., 19; nucleus of, 19; early extension of, 19; projectors of, 30; 1846 summary, 36; manifesto *re* S.-W. Rly., 80; new bills, 82: foresight of, 86; Perth Sta., 65; Greenock trains, 66; powers of other companies over, 68; Callander and Oban line, 68, 162; to Edinburgh through Holytown and W. Calder, 102; Buchanan St., Glasgow, 105; growing pains, 121; carriage of cattle, 142; of sheep, 158; grease-factory, 185; number of waggons owned by, 186
Canals, Forth and Clyde, 9; Monkland, 11–13; "Cut of Junction," 12; Ardrossan, 26; Caledonian, 72; Aberdeen and Inverurie, 119
Canobie Muir, 110
Carlisle, 110

Castlecary, 36, 37
Castle Douglas to Stranraer, 67
Cattle trade, 111–113; raising, 139; cost of carriage, 140
Causeway end, 18
Cheese, 171
City and District Rly., Glasgow, 70, 71, 159
—— of Glasgow Union Rly., 40
Clyde, the, 83; progress on, 84; steamboat traffic, 87
Coal consumption, Glasgow, 19; delivery, 20
Competition, 3; leading characteristic, 39; Gt. North and Highland, 60; key-note, 172
Connal Ferry, 162
Cowlairs Tunnel, 103
Craigellachie, 133
Craigendoran, 97

D.

DALKEITH Railway, 8
Dalwhinnie, 73; sheep, 159
Damhead, 54
Deeside line, 121, 123
Defiance, coach, 55
Devastation, the, 45
Distances, comparative, London to Perth and Aberdeen, 56; Glasgow to the Coast, 91; Perth to Wick, 74
Drumouchter Pass, 73
Dumbarton, 82
Dumfries, 7; to Castle Douglas, 67
Dundee and Newtyle Rly., 8
Dunoon, 98
Dunragit to Girvan, 171

E.

EAST COAST Rly., 60; prospects, 78, 79; carriage of cattle, 142; speed, 58, 182
Edinburgh, re Rly. stations, 106; to Carlisle, 108-110
Emigrants, 134-136
Engines, Great North, 121; Highland, 153; Caledonian, 180; Drummond's "No. 123," 32, 180
Eskdale, 110
Evan, "plane of the," vid. Beattock Bank, 32, 33; Water, 34, 35
Expresses—so-called, 102, 103

F.

FALKIRK fair, 111
Fares, Glasgow to Ayr, 89; to Wemyss Bay, 92; remarks, 93, 94; to Gourock, etc., 97, 98; to Edinburgh and Glasgow, 102; ten years ago on the Great North, 173-174
Farg, valley of the, 54
Fochabers, 133
Forres (elbow by), 74; fertile ground, 116, 117
Fort Matilda, 87
Forth Bridge — Personal impressions of, 45; model of, 46; construction of, 47; early schemes, 51; approach lines, 53; gain by route, 56; relative to Edinburgh, 108; granite, 138
Forth and Clyde canal, 9

Foxwell's, Mr., "Express trains," 61, 107
Fraserburgh, 123

G.

GAIRLOCH, 148
Gala Water, 109
Galashiels, 109
Garnkirk Rly., 19; increased traffic, 23
—— and Falkirk (planned), 25; and Caledonian, 37
Gartsherrie ironworks, 18; inn, 23
Glasgow, city of, 8; growth of, 19; means of locomotion, 84; population, 87; Chamber of Commerce, 102; stations, 103
Glasgow and S.-W. Rly., 4; vid. Perth, 64; and its ancestors, 26-28; complicated relationship with other companies, 66; its coast services, 85; a creditable train, 89; a possible extension, 97; its proposed amalgamation with N. British. See Amalgamation.
Glenfarg, 54, 55
Glenlivat, 122
Goods trains started, 22
Gordon Cathcart (Lady), 128, 135
Gourock Bay, 86
Gradients, 33, 103, 109, 114, 168, 180-2
Grand Junction open, 32
Grangemouth, 100
Great North of Scotland Rly., 4,

60, 74, 116–141; result of amalgamations, 40; signalling, 164
Great Northern *vid.* Perth, 64; *see* also East Coast, and Forth Bridge.
Greenock, 84 *et seq.*
—— to Belfast, 169
Guano, carriage of, 141

H.

HALKIRK, 155; Mr. W. L. Howie; 155, 156
Harbours, fishing, 128
Hardengreen, 129
Haymarket, cattle-market, 113
Hawick, 40, 109
Heating carriages, 178, 179
Helensburgh, 82, 85
Hell's Glen, 97
Herring fishery, 126; store, 127; kippers, 128; W. Highland, 161.
Highland Rly., 4, 5, 40, 58–62, 116; cornering, 73; extension, 74; regarding fish, 129; sheep, 142, 158; signalling, 145, 146; carriages, engines, 153

I.

IMPORTATION of cattle, 141
Inchgarvie, 45
Innellan, 86
Inveraray, 97
Inverchapel, 98
Inverness, 4, 58, 60–62, 73, 121

J.

JOHNSTONE, Mr. Hope, 32, 34
Jute, 126

K.

KEMNAY, 137
Killiecrankie, Pass of, 155
Kilwinning, Ardrossan canal, 27
Kilmarnock and Troon Rly., 6, 7
Kilsyth and Bonnybridge, 80
Kirn, watering place, 91
Kittybrewster, 120, 121
Kyles of Bute, 97

L.

LAND, value of, Glasgow, 104
Larbert, the Rly. Luxemburg, 67; lines north of, 69
Largs, steamers and trains to, 86
Leith, 101; whiskey traffic, 122
Leven, Vale of, 122
Liddesdale, 110
Linn, Walter, diary of, 21
Loch, Long, 71, 87; Tay, 71; Treig, 73; Fyne, 97; Goil, 97; Eck, 98; Lomond, 71, 98
Lochnagar, 122
Locke, Joseph, survey and report, 30, 31; his shed, 105

M.

MAILS, 58, 136-7
Manure Company, Aberdeen, 141

Markets, Edinburgh and Perth, 111
Maud Junction, 131
Mawcarse, 54
Melrose, 109
Merry, Mr., and the Great North, 118
Midland Rly., *vid.* Perth 64; to Castle Douglas, 67; to Wigtown and Portpatrick, 166, 167. *See* also under heads, Forth Bridge, distances and amalgamations.
Millerhill Junction, 108
Millport, steamers to, ferry, 86
Monkland and Kirkintilloch Rly., 9, 14; partly closed, 18; continued, 19; Rlys., 18; opened, 20
"Monumental lines," 57
Moray, 121
Mushrooms, 113–115

N.

NAIRN, 74
Netherby Hall, 110
Niddrie, 113
Nithsdale, 31
North British, 3, 18; proper territory, 19; beginning, 39; interruption, 56; self-competition, 66; as regards Forth and Tay bridges, 69; City and District Rly. (Glasgow), 70, 71; Caledonian retaliation, 82; all-absorbing, 85; *vid.* Bathgate, 102; at Edinburgh, 108; "horsed" by N.E., 108; carriage of cattle, 111–113;

lighting, 189, 190. *See* also East Coast, Forth Bridge, speed, distances, amalgamation.
North Eastern Rly., 64, 108. *See* also as above.
North-Western Rly., 64; Callander and Oban, 68; *re* Wigtownshire and Portpatrick Rly., 167. *See* also West Coast and as above.

O.

OUTING, animals' annual, 158
Outlook for the future, 39, 197.

P.

PAISLEY, 84
Panic of 1866, 86
Parcels, Glasgow and Airdrie, 22; Post, 137
Perth stat., magnitude of, 63
Peterhead, 133
Physical geography, influence of, 35
Polloc and Govan Rly., 5, 6
Portpatrick, 168, 169
Portsoy, 133
Postal subsidy, G. North, 136; Highland, 137
Princes St. Gardens, 107

Q.

QUEEN'S letter, the, 147, 141
Queen St. Stat., Glasgow, 103; electric lighting, 190

R.

Railways, competitors with, 24, 25; connecting England and Scotland, 28; projectors of 1846, 40
Railway Regulation Act, 1889, 151
Rannoch, moor of, 71
Rate for sugar, 100, 101; for fish, 130; for meat, 142
Rolling stock, American opinion on, 120
Roshven, in Moidart, 72, 73
Rothesay, 86; steamers for, 87
Russell, Scott, 24

S.

St. Catherine's, 97
St. Rollox, 19; locomotive and carriage works, 179, 185, 189
Sand-drifts, 186, 187
Sanding apparatus, 183
Sanquhar collieries, 7
Season tickets, 91
Shankend Tunnel, 109
Shunting, 149
Signalling, 148, 163-166
Skye line, 160
Slamannan Co., 18; and Bo'ness, 19
Slitrig, valley of the, 109
Snowploughs and fences, 155
Solway Moss, 110
Speed, canals and early Rlys., 35
—— between Glasgow and the Coast, 87; Edinburgh and Glasgow, 102; Edinburgh and Carlisle, 108, 110, 181; on the Great North, 119; on the Highland, 145
Speed, probable, this summer from London, 58, 182
Stations, Edinburgh, Haymarket and Waverley, 106, 107
Steam road-carriages, 25
Stephenson, Geo., 20
Strachur, 98
Stranraer, 169
Strath Avon, 122
Strome Ferry, 73, 145
Sugar-refining, 100

T.

Tain, 145
Tanning, 117
Tay Bridge, 52, 53, 182
Teviot, 109
Through route, 35; first idea of, 39
Tickets first issued, 1837, 22; through, 97
Time tables, compared, 91; Glasgow and Edinburgh, 102, 103; Aberdeen to Elgin, 119
Tomantoul, 122
Tradestown, 26
Traffic, direction of, 2; growth of passenger, 23; through Perth, 63; sheep, 73; chief revenue of Highland Rly., 74; London and Glasgow, 78; Glasgow and Leeds, 78; Greenock new Rly., 85; Isle of Arran, 86; Caledonian, 87; passenger, Glasgow to the

coast, 85-99; St. Enoch's, 105; local, Edinburgh, 108; G. North, 116; Highland, 116; whiskey, 123; tourists, 123; fish, 130, 161; cattle, 113, 140, 161; interruption of, 154; from West Highlands, 159-160; Irish, 168-170

Train, relief, 58; postal, 59; Foxwell's "Express Trains," 61, 107; mail, 62, 136; cattle, 111-113; fast, Highlands, 119; "accommodation," 143; mixed, 149; tramways, 153

Trossachs Hotel, 98

Truck-cleaning, 113

"Turkey red," 82

Tweed river, 109

U.

ULLAPOOL, 148

W.

WAGGONS of private traders, 186

Waterloo Stat., Gt. North, 118

Watt, James, 9

Waverley, route through Melrose, 8, 109

——— station, 109

Wemyss Bay Rly., 85; fares and season tickets, 92

West Coast Rly., cattle trains, 142; speed, 58, 180, 182

West Highland line, 4; its route, 71; Act passed, 73

Westinghouse pump, 183

Whales, 123-126

Wick to Perth, distance, 74

Wigtownshire and Portpatrick Rly., 66, 167

Wool market, Inverness, 159

Wright, Mr. Andrew, 139

www.ingramcontent.com/pod-product-compliance
Lightning Source LLC
Chambersburg PA
CBHW032225230426
43666CB00033B/1530